Coraline

Coraline

NEIL GAIMAN

WITH ILLUSTRATIONS BY DAVE McKEAN

WORKBOOK

Contents

뉴베리 상이란? • 6
이 책의 구성 • 8
이 책의 활용법 • 10

chapter one
quiz & words list •••••••••••••••••••••••••••••••••• 12

chapter two
quiz & words list •••••••••••••••••••••••••••••••••• 20

chapter three
quiz & words list •••••••••••••••••••••••••••••••••• 28

chapter four
quiz & words list •••••••••••••••••••••••••••••••••• 38

chapter five
quiz & words list •••••••••••••••••••••••••••••••••• 50

chapter six
quiz & words list •••••••••••••••••••••••••••••••••• 64

chapter seven
quiz & words list •••••••••••••••••••••••••••••••••• 76

chapter eight
quiz & words list •••••••••••••••••••••••••••••••••• 82

chapter nine
quiz & words list •••••••••••••••••••••••••••••••••• 98

chapter ten
quiz & words list ·································· 108

chapter eleven
quiz & words list ·································· 120

chapter twelve
quiz & words list ·································· 132

chapter thirteen
quiz & words list ·································· 142

영어원서 읽기 TIPS • 154
Answer Key • 160

'아동 도서계의 노벨상!' 미국 최고 권위의 아동 문학상

뉴베리 상(Newbery Award)은 미국 도서관 협회에서 해마다 미국 아동 문학 발전에 가장 크게 이바지한 작가에게 수여하는 아동 문학상입니다. 1922년에 시작된 이 상은 미국에서 가장 오랜 역사를 지닌 아동 문학상이자, '아동 도서계의 노벨상'이라 불릴 만큼 높은 권위를 자랑하는 상입니다.

뉴베리 상은 그 역사와 권위만큼이나 심사 기준이 까다롭기로 유명한데, 심사단은 책의 주제 의식은 물론 정보의 깊이와 스토리의 정교함, 캐릭터와 문체의 적정성 등을 꼼꼼히 평가하여 수상작을 결정합니다.

그해 최고의 작품으로 선정된 도서에게는 '뉴베리 메달(Newbery Medal)'이라고 부르는 금색 메달을 수여하며, 최종 후보에 올랐던 주목할 만한 작품들에게는 '뉴베리 아너(Newbery Honor)'라는 이름의 은색 마크를 수여합니다.

뉴베리 상을 받은 도서는 미국의 모든 도서관에 비치되어 더 많은 독자들을 만나게 되며, 대부분 수십에서 수백만 부가 판매되는 베스트셀러가 됩니다. 뉴베리 상을 수상한 작가는 그만큼 필력과 작품성을 인정받게 되어, 수상 작가의 다른 작품들 또한 수상작 못지않게 커다란 주목과 사랑을 받습니다.

왜 뉴베리 수상작인가?
쉬운 어휘로 쓰인 '검증된' 영어원서!

뉴베리 수상작들은 '검증된 원서'로 국내 영어 학습자들에게 큰 사랑을 받고 있습니다. 뉴베리 수상작이 원서 읽기에 좋은 교재인 이유는 무엇일까요?

1. 아동 문학인 만큼 어휘가 어렵지 않습니다.
2. 어렵지 않은 어휘를 사용하면서도 '문학상'을 수상한 만큼 문장의 깊이가 상당합니다.
3. 적당한 난이도의 어휘와 깊이 있는 문장으로 구성되어 있기 때문에 초등 고학년부터 성인까지, 영어 초보자부터 실력자까지 모든 영어 학습자들이 읽기에 좋습니다.

실제로 뉴베리 수상작은 국제중·특목고에서는 입시 필독서로, 대학교에서는 영어 강독 교재로 다양하고 폭넓게 활용되고 있습니다. 이런 이유로 뉴베리 수상작은 한국어 번역서보다 오히려 원서가 훨씬 많이 판매되는 기현상을 보이고 있습니다.

'베스트 오브 베스트'만을 엄선한 「뉴베리 컬렉션」

「뉴베리 컬렉션」은 뉴베리 메달 및 아너 수상작, 그리고 뉴베리 수상 작가의 유명 작품들을 엄선하여 한국 영어 학습자들을 위한 최적의 교재로 재탄생시킨 영어 원서 시리즈입니다.

1. 어휘 수준과 문장의 난이도, 분량 등 국내 영어 학습자들에게 적합한 정도를 종합적으로 검토하여 선정하였습니다.
2. 기존 원서 독자층 사이의 인기도까지 감안하여 최적의 작품들을 선별하였습니다.
3. 판형이 좁고 글씨가 작아 읽기 힘들었던 원서 디자인을 대폭 수정하여, 판형을 시원하게 키우고 읽기에 최적화된 영문 서체를 사용하여 가독성을 극대화하였습니다.
4. 함께 제공되는 워크북은 어려운 어휘를 완벽하게 정리하고 이해력을 점검하는 퀴즈를 덧붙여 독자들이 원서를 보다 쉽고 재미있게 읽을 수 있도록 구성하였습니다.
5. 기존에 높은 가격에 판매되어 구입이 부담스러웠던 오디오북을 부록으로 제공하여 리스닝과 소리 내어 읽기에까지 원서를 두루 활용할 수 있도록 했습니다.

닐 게이먼(Neil Gaiman)은 영국 작가로, 이상하고도 엉뚱한 세상을 보여주는 판타지 문학의 소설가입니다. 그의 대표작인 「코렐라인(Coraline)」은 애니메이션으로 제작되어 전 세계적인 사랑을 받았고 국내에서도 번역 출간되었습니다. 또다른 소설 「Stardust」와 「Neverwhere」는 영화와 드라마로 제작되어 큰 인기를 얻었습니다. 그는 「코렐라인」으로 판타지 문학상인 휴고상(Hugo Awards), 네뷸러상(Nebula Awards) 등을 수상하였고, 「The Graveyard Book」으로 미국 최고 권위의 아동 문학상인 뉴베리 메달(Newbery Medal)과 영국 도서관 협회의 아동 문학상인 카네기 메달(Carnegie Medal)을 모두 수상하였습니다.

「Coraline」은 닐 게이먼이 실수로 캐롤라인(Caroline)의 'a'와 'o'를 바꿔 쓰면서 만들어 낸 독특한 캐릭터 코렐라인(Coraline)의 신비로운 모험을 그려낸 작품입니다. 영국 고대 건축 양식으로 지어진 오래된 다세대 주택으로 이사를 온 주인공 코렐라인은 새 집을 탐방하던 중 하나의 문을 발견하게 됩니다. 그러던 어느 날 집에 혼자 남겨진 코렐라인이 호기심을 가지고 그 문을 열고 들어가면서부터 그녀의 모험이 시작됩니다. 그곳에는 코렐라인 부모님의 모습을 하고 있는 또 다른 엄마, 아빠가 살고 있습니다. 그들은 진짜 부모님보다 훨씬 상냥하고 코렐라인에게 애정을 쏟아줍니다. 또 다른 엄마는 코렐라인에게 자신의 모습처럼 눈에 단추를 달고 여기 남아서 함께 행복하게 지내자고 제안합니다. 하지만 그곳에 진짜 부모님과 이미 귀신이 되어버린 몇몇 아이들이 갇혀 있음을 알게 되고, 코렐라인은 탈출을 위해 다른 엄마에게 내기를 겁니다. 코렐라인의 흥미진진한 모험을 따라가다 보면 독자들은 그녀의 대담한 용기와 도전 정신에 탄성을 내지르게 됩니다.

뉴베리상 수상 작가 닐 게이먼의 대표 작품인 이 책은 판타지 문학에 수여하는 네 가지 상(휴고상, 네뷸러상, 로커스상, 브램 스토커상)을 모두 석권한 작품입니다. 수상 경력이 보여주듯이 이 작품은 스토리 구성이 탄탄하고, 내용 전개가 잘 이루어져 있습니다.

이 책의 구성

원서 본문

내용이 담긴 원서 본문입니다.
원어민이 읽는 일반 원서와 같은 텍스트지만, 암기해야 할 중요 어휘들은 볼드체로 표시되어 있습니다. 이 어휘들은 지금 들고 계신 워크북에 챕터별로 정리되어 있습니다.

학습 심리학 연구 결과에 따르면, 한 단어씩 따로 외우는 단어 암기는 거의 효과가 없다고 합니다. 단어를 제대로 외우기 위해서는 문맥(Context) 속에서 단어를 암기해야 하며, 한 단어당 문맥 속에서 15번 이상 마주칠 때 완벽하게 암기할 수 있다고 합니다.

이 책의 본문에서는 중요 어휘를 볼드체로 강조하여, 문맥 속의 단어들을 더 확실히 인지(Word Cognition in Context)하도록 돕고 있습니다. 또한 대부분의 중요 단어들은 다른 챕터에서도 반복해서 등장하기 때문에 이 책을 읽는 것만으로도 자연스럽게 어휘력을 향상시킬 수 있습니다.

또한 본문 하단에는 내용 이해를 돕기 위한 '각주'가 첨가되어 있습니다. 각주는 굳이 암기할 필요는 없지만, 알아 두면 도움이 될 만한 정보를 설명하고 있습니다. 각주를 참고하면 스토리를 더 깊이 있게 이해할 수 있어 원서를 읽는 재미가 배가됩니다.

워크북(Workbook)

Check Your Reading Speed
해당 챕터의 단어 수가 기록되어 있어, 리딩 속도를 측정할 수 있습니다. 특히 리딩 속도를 중시하는 독자들이 유용하게 사용할 수 있습니다.

Build Your Vocabulary
본문에 볼드 표시되어 있던 단어들이 정리되어 있습니다. 리딩 전·후에 반복해서 보면 원서를 더욱 쉽게 읽을 수 있고, 어휘력도 빠르게 향상될 것입니다.

단어는 〈스펠링 – 빈도 – 발음기호 – 품사 – 한글 뜻 – 영문 뜻〉 순서로 표기되어 있으며 빈도 표시(★)가 많을수록 필수 어휘입니다. 반복해서 등장하는 단어는 빈도 대신 '복습'으로 표기되어 있습니다. 품사는 아래와 같이 표기했습니다.

n. 명사 | a. 형용사 | ad. 부사 | vi. 자동사 | vt. 타동사 | v. 자·타동사 모두 쓰이는 동사
conj. 접속사 | prep. 전치사 | int. 감탄사 | phrasal v. 구동사 | idiom 숙어 및 관용구

Comprehension Quiz
간단한 퀴즈를 통해 읽은 내용에 대한 이해력을 점검해 볼 수 있습니다.

「뉴베리 컬렉션」 이렇게 읽어 보세요!

아래와 같이 프리뷰(Preview) → 리딩(Reading) → 리뷰(Review) 세 단계를 거치면서
읽으면, 더욱 효과적으로 영어 실력을 향상할 수 있습니다.

1. 프리뷰(Preview) : 오늘 읽을 내용을 먼저 점검하자!

* 워크북을 통해 오늘 읽을 챕터에 나와 있는 단어들을 쭉 훑어봅니다. 어떤 단
  어들이 나오는지, 내가 아는 단어와 모르는 단어는 어떤 것들이 있는지 가벼운
  마음으로 살펴봅니다.
* 평소처럼 하나하나 쓰면서 암기하려고 하지는 마세요! 익숙하지 않은 단어들
  을 주의 깊게 보되, 어차피 리딩을 하면시 점차 익숙해질 단어라는 것을 기억
  하며 빠르게 훑어봅니다.
* 뒤 챕터로 갈수록 '복습'이라고 표시된 단어들이 늘어나는 것을 알 수 있습니
  다. '복습' 단어인데도 여전히 익숙하지 않다면 더욱 신경을 써서 봐야겠죠? 매
  일매일 꾸준히 읽는다면, 익숙한 단어들이 점점 많아진다는 것을 몸으로 느낄
  수 있습니다.

2. 리딩(Reading) : 내용에 집중하며 빠르게 읽어 나가자!

* 프리뷰를 마친 후 바로 리딩을 시작합니다. 방금 살펴봤던 어휘들을 문장 속에
  서 다시 만나게 되는데, 이 과정에서 단어의 쓰임새와 어감을 자연스럽게 익히
  게 됩니다.
* 모르는 단어나 이해되지 않는 문장이 나오더라도 멈추지 말고 전체적인 맥락
  을 파악하면서 속도감 있게 읽어 나가세요. 이해되지 않는 문장들은 따로 표시
  를 하되, 일단 넘어가고 계속 읽는 것이 좋습니다. 뒷부분을 읽다 보면 자연히
  이해가 되는 경우도 있고, 정 이해가 되지 않는 부분은 리딩을 마친 이후에 따
  로 리뷰하는 시간을 가지면 됩니다. 문제집을 풀듯이 모든 문장을 분석하면서
  원서를 읽는 것이 아니라, 리딩을 할 때는 리딩에만, 리뷰를 할 때는 리뷰에만
  집중하는 것이 필요합니다.
* 볼드 처리된 단어의 의미가 궁금하더라도 워크북을 바로 펼치지 마세요. 정 궁
  금하다면 한 번씩 참고하는 것도 나쁘진 않지만, 워크북과 원서를 번살아 보면
  서 읽는 것은 리딩의 흐름을 끊고 단어 하나하나에 집착하는 좋지 않은 리딩
  습관을 심어 줄 수 있습니다.
* 같은 맥락에서 번역서를 구해 원서와 동시에 번갈아 보는 것도 좋은 방법이 아
  닙니다. 한글 번역을 가지고 있다고 해도 일단 영어로 읽을 때는 영어에만 집
  중하고 어느 정도 분량을 읽은 후에 번역서와 비교하도록 하세요. 모든 문장을
  일일이 번역해서 완벽하게 이해하려는 것은 오히려 좋지 않은 리딩 습관을 심

어 주어 장기적으로는 바람직하지 않은 결과를 얻을 수 있습니다. 처음부터 완벽하게 이해하려고 하는 것보다는 빠른 속도로 2~3회 반복해서 읽는 방식이 실력 향상에 더 도움이 됩니다. 만일 반복해서 읽어도 내용이 전혀 이해되지 않아 곤란하다면 책 선정에 문제가 있다고 할 수 있습니다. 그럴 때는 좀 더 쉬운 책을 골라 실력을 다진 뒤 다시 도전하는 것이 좋습니다.

- 초보자라면 분당 150단어의 리딩 속도를 목표로 잡고 리딩을 합니다. 분당 150단어는 원어민이 말하는 속도로, 영어 학습자들이 리스닝과 스피킹으로 넘어가기 위해 가장 기초적으로 달성해야 하는 단계입니다. 분당 50~80단어 정도의 낮은 리딩 속도를 가지고 있는 경우는 대부분 영어 실력이 부족해서라기보다 '잘못된 리딩 습관'을 가지고 있어서 그렇습니다. 이해력이 조금 떨어진다고 하더라도 분당 150단어까지는 속도에 대한 긴장감을 놓치지 말고 속도감 있게 읽어 나가도록 하세요.

3. 리뷰(Review) : 이해력을 점검하고 꼼꼼하게 다시 살펴보자!

- 해당 챕터의 Comprehension Quiz를 통해 이해력을 점검해 봅니다.
- 오늘 만난 어휘들을 다시 한번 복습합니다. 이때는 읽으면서 중요하다고 생각했던 단어를 연습장에 써 보면서 꼼꼼하게 외우는 것도 좋습니다.
- 이해가 되지 않는다고 표시해 두었던 부분도 주의 깊게 분석해 봅니다. 다시 한번 문장을 꼼꼼히 읽고, 어떤 이유에서 이해가 되지 않았는지 생각해 봅니다. 따로 메모를 남기거나 노트를 작성하는 것도 좋은 방법입니다.
- 사실 꼼꼼히 리뷰하는 것은 매우 고된 과정입니다. 원서를 읽고 리뷰하는 시간을 가지는 것이 영어 실력 향상에 많은 도움이 되기는 하지만, 이 과정을 철저히 지키려다가 원서 읽기의 재미를 반감시키는 것은 바람직하지 않습니다. 그럴 때는 차라리 리뷰를 가볍게 하는 것이 좋을 수 있습니다. '내용에 빠져서 재미있게', 문제집에서는 상상도 못할 '많은 양'을 읽으면서, 매일매일 조금씩 꾸준히 실력을 키워 가는 것이 원서를 활용하는 기본적인 방법이며, 영어 공부의 왕도입니다. 문제집 풀듯이 원서 읽기를 시도하고 접근해서는 실패할 수밖에 없습니다.
- 이런 방식으로 원서를 끝까지 다 읽었다면, 다시 반복해서 읽거나 오디오북을 활용하는 등 다양한 방식으로 원서 읽기를 확장해 나갈 수 있습니다. 이에 대한 자세한 안내가 워크북 말미에 실려 있습니다.

chapter one

1. Why did Coraline's family share the house with others?
   A. The house was a theater and had many actors for performances.
   B. The house was large and they owned just a part of it.
   C. The others living there were close family friends.
   D. Coraline's family wanted Coraline to have many friends her own age.

2. What similar thing happened when Coraline first met Miss Spink and Miss Forcible and then again with the old man with the mustache?
   A. Coraline received presents to welcome her to the house.
   B. Coraline watched their art performances.
   C. Coraline corrected their pronunciation of her name.
   D. Coraline asked them to show her around the house.

3. How did Coraline first feel about the old man's mouse circus?
   A. She didn't believe that there was a mouse circus.
   B. She wanted to see the mouse circus.
   C. She thought the mice needed more time to practice.
   D. She felt that it was mean toward the mice.

4. Why did Coraline want to find the well?

   A. It sounded exciting, so she wanted to play around it.

   B. She wanted to know where it was in order to be safer.

   C. She thought there might be interesting animals around it.

   D. She just wanted to see how deep it could go.

5. How did Coraline spend her first two weeks in the house?

   A. She watched TV and read books inside.

   B. She explored the garden and grounds of the house.

   C. She helped her parents with their work.

   D. She searched for a secret, hidden door inside the house.

6. Why was Coraline usually NOT allowed in the drawing room?

   A. Her father kept his drawing supplies there and needed it for his work.

   B. It was under construction and dangerous.

   C. It was only used for guests visiting their family.

   D. Her parents kept her grandmother's expensive furniture there.

7. Why didn't Coraline's mother lock the door in the drawing room?

   A. She had lost the key.

   B. The door was broken and wouldn't shut.

   C. It was bricked up and didn't go anywhere.

   D. Coraline wanted to go back to see it later.

1분에 몇 단어를 읽는지 리딩 속도를 측정해보세요.

$$\frac{1,926 \text{ words}}{\text{reading time (\quad) sec}} \times 60 = (\qquad) \text{ WPM}$$

Build Your Vocabulary

attic*
[ǽtik]

n. 다락(방), 지붕밑 방
An attic is a room at the top of a house just below the roof.

cellar*
[sélər]

n. 지하 저장실
A cellar is a room underneath a building, which is often used for storing things in.

overgrow
[òuvərgróu]

vt. (잡초 등이) 자라서 뒤덮다, 무성하게 자라다; 너무 커지다
(overgrown a. 마구 자란)
If a place is overgrown, it is thickly covered with plants because it has not been looked after.

flat**
[flæt]

① n. (연립주택, 다세대 주택 등을 포함하는) 아파트식 주거지
② a. 평평한, 균일한; 단호한; n. 평지, 평원
A flat is a set of rooms for living in, usually on one floor and part of a larger building. A flat usually includes a kitchen and bathroom.

tread the boards

idiom 무대에 서다, 배우가 되다
When someone treads the boards, they perform on stage in a theater.

up all night

idiom 밤을 꼬박 지새우다
If you were up all night, you couldn't sleep throughout the night.

tummy
[tʌ́mi]

n. 배
Your tummy is the part of the front of your body below your waist.

mustache*
[mʌ́stæʃ]

n. 코밑수염
A man's mustache is the hair that grows on his upper lip.

wonder***
[wʌ́ndə:r]

n. 경탄할 만한 것, 경이; v. 호기심을 가지다, 이상하게 여기다
If you say that it is a wonder that something happened, you mean that it is very surprising and unexpected.

rehearse
[rihə́:rs]

v. 연습하다, ~의 예행연습을 하다
If you rehearse something that you are going to say or do, you silently practice it by imagining that you are saying or doing it.

make up

phrasal v. (이야기 따위를) 지어내다; 만들다, 구성하다
If you make something up, you invent it, such as an excuse or a story, often in order to trick someone.

explore*
[iksplɔ́:r]

v. 탐험[답사] 하다, 탐구하다, 조사하다
If you explore a place, you travel around it to find out what it is like.

14

rot*
[rat]

v. 썩다, 썩이다; n. 썩음, 부패
When food, wood, or another substance rots, or when something rots it, it becomes softer and is gradually destroyed.

stunt*
[stʌnt]

① v. 성장[발달]을 방해[저해]하다; n. 성장이 저해된 생물;
② v. 묘기를 부리다; n. 묘기, 곡예
If something stunts the growth or development of a person or thing, it prevents it from growing or developing as much as it should.

flyblow
[fláiblòu]

v. (flyblew–flyblown) (파리가) 쉬를 슬다, 구더기가 생기다; n. 구더기
To flyblow means to contaminate.

rosebush
[rouzbùʃ]

n. 장미 관목[덩굴]
Rosebush is the shrub that roses grow on, a rose plant.

squidgy
[skwídʒi]

a. (땅 등이) 질척한
Something that is squidgy is soft and can be squashed easily.

dreadful*
[drédfəl]

a. 지독한; 무서운, 두려운
If you say that something is dreadful, you mean that it is very bad or unpleasant, or very poor in quality.

accidental*
[æksədéntl]

a. 우연한; 부수적인 (accidentally ad. 우연히)
An accidental event happens by chance or as the result of an accident, and is not deliberately intended.

tread*
[tred]

v. (trod–trod/trodden) 밟다, 걷다; n. 밟기, 걷기; 발판, 페달, 접촉면
If you tread in a particular way, you walk that way.

well*
[wel]

n. 우물; v. 솟아 나오다, 내뿜다, 분출하다
A well is a hole in the ground from which a supply of water is extracted.

warn***
[wɔːrn]

v. 경고하다; ~에게 통지[통고]하다
If you warn someone about something such as a possible danger or problem, you tell them about it so that they are aware of it.

set off

phrasal v. 시작하다, 착수하다, 출발하다; (알람 등이) 울리다
When you set off to do something, you begin doing it.

proper***
[prápər]

a. 적당[타당]한; 예의 바른; 고유의 (properly ad. 적당히, 알맞게)
The proper thing is the one that is correct or most suitable.

meadow*
[médou]

n. 목초지, 초원
A meadow is a field which has grass and flowers growing in it.

clump
[klʌmp]

n. 수풀, (관목의) 덤불
A clump of things such as trees or plants is a small group of them growing together.

pebble*
[pebl]

n. 조약돌, 자갈
A pebble is a small, smooth, round stone which is found on beaches and at the bottom of rivers.

acorn
[éikɔːrn]

n. 도토리
An acorn is a pale oval nut that is the fruit of an oak tree.

hedgehog
[hédʒhɔ̀g]

n. [동물] 고슴도치
A hedgehog is a small brown animal with sharp spikes covering its back.

toad[*]
[toud]

n. [동물] 두꺼비
A toad is a creature which is similar to a frog but which has a drier skin and spends less time in water.

haughty
[hɔ́ːti]

a. 오만한, 거만한
You use haughty to describe someone's behavior or appearance when you disapprove of the fact that they seem to be very proud and to think that they are better than other people.

stump[*]
[stʌmp]

n. (나무의) 그루터기; 잘리고 남은 부분; vt. (발부리를) 차이다
A stump is a small part of something that remains when the rest of it has been removed or broken off.

slip[*]
[slip]

v. 살짝 나오다[들어가다]; 미끄러지다; 슬며시 두다
(slip away phrasal v. 슬그머니 떠나다)
If you slip somewhere, you go there quickly and quietly.

if ever

idiom 설사 ~하는 일이 있다 해도
You use if ever with past tenses when you are introducing a description of a person or thing, to emphasize how appropriate it is.

pester
[péstər]

vt. 괴롭히다, 못살게 굴다, 고통을 주다; n. 훼방, 방해
If you say that someone is pestering you, you mean that they keep asking you to do something, or keep talking to you, and you find this annoying.

mess[*]
[mes]

n. 엉망진창, 난잡함; v. 망쳐놓다, 방해하다
If you say that something is a mess or in a mess, you think that it is in an untidy state.

splash[*]
[splæʃ]

v. (물 · 흙탕물을) 튀(기)다, 첨벙거리다; n. 첨벙 하는 소리; (잉크 등의) 방울, 얼룩
If you splash a liquid somewhere or if it splashes, it hits someone or something and scatters in a lot of small drops.

mean business

idiom 진심이다, 진지하다
If you say that someone means business, you mean they are serious and determined about what they are doing.

current[**]
[kə́ːrənt]

a. 지금의, 현재의; 유행하는; n. 해류, 기류; 흐름 (currently ad. 현재, 지금)
Current means happening, being used, or being done at the present time.

muddy[*]
[mʌ́di]

a. 진흙의; 흐린, 탁한
Something that is muddy contains mud or is covered in mud.

eventually[**]
[ivéntʃuəli]

ad. 결국, 마침내
Eventually means at the end of a situation or process or as the final result of it.

protect[**]
[prətékt]

v. 보호하다, 막다, 지키다 (protective a. 지키는, 보호하는)
To protect someone or something means to prevent them from being harmed or damaged.

16

coloration
[kʌləréiʃən]

n. (생물의) 천연색
The coloration of an animal or a plant is the colors and patterns on it.

disguise*
[disgáiz]

vt. 변장[위장]시키다; n. 변장, 위장
If you disguise yourself, you put on clothes which make you look like someone else or alter your appearance in other ways, so that people will not recognize you.

twig*
[twig]

n. 잔가지, 가는 가지
A twig is a very small thin branch that grows out from a main branch of a tree or bush.

bucket*
[bʌkit]

v. (비가) 억수로 퍼붓다; 양동이로 물을 긷다[붓다]; n. 양동이, 버킷
To bucket down means to pour down heavily.

carry on

phrasal v. (임무·일을) 계속하다, (중단된 일 등을) 재개하다
If you carry on doing something, you continue or persevere in doing it.

mount*
[maunt]

v. (~을 조직하여) 시작하다; 오르다, 올라타다; 설치하다, 탑재하다
If you mount a campaign or event, you organize it and make it take place.

expedition*
[èkspədíʃən]

n. 원정, (탐험 등의) 여행
An expedition is an organized journey that is made for a particular purpose such as exploration.

consider***
[kənsídər]

v. 고려하다, 숙고하다
If you consider something, you think about it carefully.

cupboard*
[kʌbərd]

n. 식기장, 찬장; 붙박이장, 벽장
A cupboard is a piece of furniture that has one or two doors, usually contains shelves, and is used to store things.

carve*
[kɑːrv]

vt. 새기다, 조각하다
If you carve an object, you make it by cutting it out of a substance such as wood or stone.

string**
[striŋ]

n. 끈, 줄, 실; v. 묶다, 매달다, 꿰다
A string of things is a number of them on a piece of string, thread, or wire.

doorframe
[dɔ́ːrfrèim]

n. 문틀
A doorframe is a frame that supports a door.

sort***
[sɔːrt]

vt. 분류하다, 골라내다; n. 종류, 부류
If you sort things, you separate them into different classes, groups, or places, for example so that you can do different things with them.

rust**
[rʌst]

v. (금속 등이) 녹슬다, 부식하다; n. 녹 (rusty a. 녹슨)
If metal rusts or something rusts it, it becomes covered with a brown substance when it contacts with water.

swing**
[swiŋ]

v. (swung–swung) 휙 돌리다, 회전시키다, 빙 돌다; 휘두르다, 흔들다; 매달리다
If something swings in a particular direction or if you swing it in that direction, it moves in that direction with a smooth, curving movement.

shrug*
[ʃrʌg]

v. (양 손바닥을 내보이면서 어깨를) 으쓱하다; n. 으쓱하기
If you shrug, you raise your shoulders to show that you are not interested in something or that you do not know or care about something.

patter
[pǽtər]

v. 후두두[타닥타닥] 하는 소리를 내다; (발걸음을) 가볍게 걸어가다; n. 후두두[타닥타닥] 하는 소리
If something patters on a surface, it hits the surface quickly several times, making quiet, tapping sounds.

blur
[bləːr]

v. (광경·의식·눈 등을) 흐리게 하다; n. 흐림, 침침함; 더러움, 얼룩
When a thing blurs or when something blurs it, you cannot see it clearly because its edges are no longer distinct.

disgust*
[disgʌst]

vt. 역겹게 하다, 넌더리나게 하다; n. 싫음, 혐오감
(disgusted a. 혐오감을 느끼는)
To disgust someone means to make them feel a strong sense of dislike and disapproval.

recipe**
[résəpiː]

n. (요리의) 조리법; (약제 등의) 처방전
A recipe is a list of ingredients and a set of instructions that tell you how to cook something.

stew*
[stjuː]

n. 스튜 (요리); v. [약한] 불로 끓(이)다
A stew is a meal which you make by cooking meat and vegetables in liquid at a low temperature.

admit***
[ədmít]

v. 인정하다
If you admit that something bad, unpleasant, or embarrassing is true, you agree, often unwillingly, that it is true.

freezer*
[fríːzər]

n. 냉동고
A freezer is a large container like a fridge in which the temperature is kept below freezing point so that you can store food inside it for long periods.

lie***
[lai]

vi. (lay-lain) 눕다, 누워 있다; 놓여 있다, 위치하다
If you are lying somewhere, you are in a horizontal position and are not standing or sitting.

snore*
[snɔːr]

v. 코를 골다; n. 코 고는 소리
When someone who is asleep snores, they make a loud noise each time they breathe.

occasional*
[əkéiʒənl]

a. 가끔의, 때때로의
Occasional means happening sometimes, but not regularly or often.

mutter*
[mʌtər]

n. 중얼거림, 불평; v. 중얼거리다, 불평하다
A mutter is a soft, barely audible or indistinct tone of voice.

scuttle
[skʌtl]

vi. 급히 가다, 황급히 달리다; 허둥지둥 도망가다
When people or small animals scuttle somewhere, they run there with short quick steps.

patch*
[pætʃ]

n. 부분, 단편, 파편; 헝겊 조각; 반창고; v. 헝겊을 대고 깁다
A patch on a surface is a part of it which is different in appearance from the area around it.

18

intense*
[inténs]

a. 강렬한, 격렬한, 심한 (intensely ad. 강렬하게, 격하게)
Intense is used to describe something that is very great or extreme in strength or degree.

doorway*
[dɔ́:rwèi]

n. 문간, 현관, 출입구
A doorway is a space in a wall where a door opens and closes.

cast***
[kæst]

v. (cast–cast) (그림자 따위를) 드리우다; 내던지다; 배역을 정하다; n. 깁스, 붕대
If something casts a light or shadow somewhere, it causes it to appear there.

distort
[distɔ́:rt]

vt. (얼굴 등을) 찡그리다, 찌푸리다; 비틀다; 왜곡하다
(distorted a. 찌그러진, 일그러진)
If someone's face or body distorts or is distorted, it moves into an unnatural and unattractive shape or position.

edge**
[edʒ]

n. 가장자리, 변두리, 끝; v. 조금씩[살살] 움직이다[이동시키다]; 테두리를 두르다
The edge of something is the place or line where it stops, or the part of it that is furthest from the middle.

pause**
[pɔ:z]

vi. 중단하다, 잠시 멈추다; n. 멈춤, 중지
If you pause while you are doing something, you stop for a short period and then continue.

dash*
[dæʃ]

v. 돌진하다; 내던지다; n. 돌격; 소량
If you dash somewhere, you run or go there quickly and suddenly.

farthest**
[fɑ́:rðist]

a. (far–farther–farthest) 가장 먼; ad. 가장 멀리(에)
Something farthest is at the greatest distance in space, direction or time.

crack**
[kræk]

n. 조금, 약간; 갈라진 금; 갑작스런 날카로운 소리; v. 금이 가다, 깨다, 부수다
If you open something such as a door, window, or curtain a crack, you open it only a small amount.

slide*
[slaid]

v. (slid–slid) 미끄러지다, 미끄러지듯 움직이다
If you slide somewhere, you move there smoothly and quietly.

avoid***
[əvɔ́id]

vt. 피하다, 막다
If you avoid a person or thing, you keep away from them.

gather**
[gǽðər]

v. 모이다, 모으다
If people gather somewhere or if someone gathers people somewhere, they come together in a group.

whisper*
[hwíspə:r]

v. 속삭이다
When you whisper, you say something very quietly.

whine
[hwain]

v. 우는소리를 하다, 푸념하다; 윙 소리를 내다; n. 윙 소리; 흐느낌
(whiney a. 우는 소리를 하는, 투덜대는)
If something or someone whines, they make a long, high-pitched noise, especially one which sounds sad or unpleasant.

commercial**
[kəmə́:rʃəl]

n. (텔레비전 · 라디오의) 광고 (방송); a. 상업의, 무역의
A commercial is an advertisement that is broadcast on television or radio.

chapter two

1. How did Miss Spink describe the fog surrounding the house after the rain?
   A. She said it was terrific weather.
   B. She said it was boring weather.
   C. She said it was rotten weather.
   D. She said it was refreshing weather.

2. Why was Miss Forcible worried about Miss Spink?
   A. She was worried that Miss Spink might ruin her clothing.
   B. She was worried that Miss Spink might get lost and get sick.
   C. She was worried that Miss Spink might lose the dogs.
   D. She was worried that Miss Spink might fall in the well.

3. What message did the mice have for Coraline?
   A. Don't go through the door.
   B. Come see the circus.
   C. Don't get sick.
   D. Be careful of the old man.

4. How did Coraline think the door in the drawing room might have been locked?

   A. The dogs might have escaped, so Miss Forcible might have locked it.

   B. It might have locked itself.

   C. Coraline's father might have locked it.

   D. Coraline's mother might have locked it.

5. What did Miss Spink and Miss Forcible read in Coraline's tea leaves?

   A. Coraline will be blessed with fortune.

   B. Coraline will do well in school next week.

   C. Coraline is in danger.

   D. Coraline's parents will get terribly sick.

6. What did Coraline receive from Miss Spink?

   A. A thimble for sewing.

   B. A china duck for good luck.

   C. A brass coin to buy candy.

   D. A stone with a hole in it.

1분에 몇 단어를 읽는지 리딩 속도를 측정해보세요.

$$\frac{1,470 \text{ words}}{\text{reading time ( ) sec}} \times 60 = (\quad) \text{ WPM}$$

Build Your Vocabulary

fog**
[fɔːg]

n. 안개; 혼란
When there is fog, there are tiny drops of water in the air which form a thick cloud and make it difficult to see things.

hood*
[hud]

n. 두건; 자동차 보닛, 덮개
A hood is a part of a coat which you can pull up to cover your head. It is in the shape of a triangular bag attached to the neck of the coat at the back.

rot^{복습}
[rɑt]

v. 썩다, 썩이다; n. 썩음, 부패 (rotten a. 형편없는, 끔찍한; 썩은)
When food, wood, or another substance rots, or when something rots it, it becomes softer and is gradually destroyed.

tread the boards^{복습}

idiom 무대에 서다, 배우가 되다
When someone treads the boards, they perform on stage in a theater.

bundle (someone) up

phrasal v. ~을 따뜻하게 둘러싸다
If you bundle someone up, you make them feel warmer by putting warm clothes on them or covering them with blankets.

cardigan
[kɑ́ːrdigən]

n. 카디건(단추 달린 스웨터)
A cardigan is a knitted woollen sweater that you can fasten at the front with buttons or a zip.

circular*
[sə́ːrkjələr]

a. 원의, 원형의
Something that is circular is shaped like a circle.

fluffy
[flʌfi]

a. 푹신한, 보풀의, 솜털의
If you describe something such as a towel or a toy animal as fluffy, you mean that it is very soft.

cautious*
[kɔ́ːʃəs]

a. 조심성 있는, 신중한 (cautiously ad. 조심스럽게)
Someone who is cautious acts very carefully in order to avoid possible danger.

peer*
[piər]

vi. 응시하다, 자세히 보다
If you peer at something, you look at it very hard.

mist**
[mist]

n. 안개; v. 안개가 끼다, 눈이 흐려지다
Mist consists of a large number of tiny drops of water in the air, which make it difficult to see very far.

whisper^{복습}
[hwíspəːr]

v. 속삭이다
When you whisper, you say something very quietly.

tug[*] [tʌg]	**v.** (세게) 당기다, 끌다; 노력[분투]하다; **n.** 힘껏 당김; 분투, 노력 If you tug something or tug at it, you give it a quick and usually strong pull.
to heel	**idiom** 바로 뒤에; 지배되어, 정복되어 If you bring someone to heel, you take them just behind you.
waddle [wadl]	**vi.** 뒤뚱거리며 걷다, 흔들 흔들거리며 가다; **n.** 뒤뚱거리는 걸음걸이 To waddle somewhere means to walk there with short, quick steps, swinging slightly from side to side.
flat[복습] [flæt]	① **n.** (연립주택, 다세대 주택 등을 포함하는) 아파트식 주거지 ② **a.** 평평한, 균일한; 단호한; **n.** 평지, 평원 A flat is a set of rooms for living in, usually on one floor and part of a larger building. A flat usually includes a kitchen and bathroom.
bring on	**phrasal v.** ~을 초래하다 If one thing brings on something, it makes something happen, usually something bad.
explorer[*] [ikspló:rər]	**n.** 탐험가; 조사자, 검사자 An explorer is someone who travels to places about which very little is known, in order to discover what is there.
limp [limp]	**a.** 약한, 기운이 없는; 흐느적거리는 If someone is limp, their body has no strength and is not moving.
damp[*] [dæmp]	**a.** 축축한; **n.** 습기 Something that is damp is slightly wet.
hardly[***] [háːrdli]	**ad.** 거의 ~아니다, 전혀 ~않다 When you say you can hardly do something, you are emphasizing that it is very difficult for you to do it.
whisker[*] [wískə:r]	**n.** (고양이 · 쥐 등의) 수염; 구레나룻 The whiskers of an animal such as a cat or a mouse are the long stiff hairs that grow near its mouth.
droop[*] [druːp]	**v.** 축 처지다, 시들다; 수그러지다 If something droops, it hangs or leans downward with no strength or firmness.
admit[복습] [ədmít]	**v.** 인정하다 If you admit that something bad, unpleasant, or embarrassing is true, you agree, often unwillingly, that it is true.
lean[**] [liːn]	① **v.** 상체를 굽히다, 기울다; 의지하다; ~을 기대어 세우다 ② **a.** 야윈, 마른 When you lean in a particular direction, you bend your body in that direction.
mustache[복습] [mʌ́stæʃ]	**n.** 코밑수염 A man's mustache is the hair that grows on his upper lip.
tickle[*] [tikl]	**vt.** 간지럼을 태우다, 간질이다; **n.** 간지럼 If a part of the body tickles, or if something tickles it, it feels slightly uncomfortable and you want to rub it.

pause^{복습}
[pɔ:z]

vi. 잠시 멈추다, 중단하다; n. 멈춤, 중지
If you pause while you are doing something, you stop for a short period and then continue.

shrug^{복습}
[ʃrʌg]

v. (양 손바닥을 내보이면서 어깨를) 으쓱하다; n. 으쓱하기
If you shrug, you raise your shoulders to show that you are not interested in something or that you do not know or care about something.

attic^{복습}
[ǽtik]

n. 다락(방), 지붕밑 방
An attic is a room at the top of a house just below the roof.

indoors^{★★}
[indɔ́:rz]

ad. 실내로, 실내에서
If something happens indoors, it happens inside a building.

remind^{★★}
[rimáind]

vt. 생각나게 하다, 상기시키다, 일깨우다
If someone reminds you of a fact or event that you already know about, they say something which makes you think about it.

wiggle
[wigl]

v. (몸을) 뒤흔들다, (좌우로) 움직이다; n. 뒤흔듦
(wiggly a. 흔들리는, 파동치는; 몸부림치는)
If you wiggle something or if it wiggles, it moves up and down or from side to side in small quick movements.

grunt[★]
[grʌnt]

vi. (사람이) 툴툴거리다; (돼지가) 꿀꿀거리다; n. 꿀꿀[툴툴]거리는 소리
If you grunt, you make a low sound, especially because you are annoyed or not interested in something.

modern^{★★}
[mɑ́dərn]

a. (예술·문학·음악 등이) 새로운, 현대적인; 현대의, 근대의
Something that is modern is new and involves the latest ideas or equipment.

creep[★]
[kri:p]

vi. (crept–crept) 천천히[살금살금] 걷다, 기다; n. 포복
If something creeps somewhere, it moves very slowly.

frenzy
[frénzi]

vi. 격분[광란]하게 하다; n. 격분, 열광, 광란 (frenzied a. 광적인, 흥분한)
If you are frenzied by something, it makes you extremely angry.

woof
[wu:f]

vi. (개가) 으르렁거리다, 비명을 지르다; n. 으르렁 하는 소리, 비명
If a dog woofs, it makes a low gruff sound.

polish^{★★}
[pɑ́liʃ]

n. 광택제; 광택, 세련; v. 닦다, 윤내다
Polish is a substance that you put on the surface of an object in order to clean it, protect it, and make it shine.

parlor^{★★}
[pɑ́:rlər]

n. 거실, 응접실; 영업실
A parlor is a room in a house where people can sit and talk and relax.

frame^{★★}
[freim]

n. 액자, 틀; 구조, 골격; vt. ~의 뼈대를 만들다, 짜 맞추다
The frame of a picture or mirror is the wood, metal, or plastic that is fitted around it, especially when it is displayed or hung on a wall.

armchair
[ɑ:rmʧɛ̀ər]

n. 안락의자, 팔걸이 의자
An armchair is a big comfortable chair which has a support on each side for your arms.

24

knit*
[nit]

v. (실로 옷 등을) 뜨다, 짜다
If you knit something, especially an article of clothing, you make it from wool or a similar thread by using two knitting needles or a machine.

saucer*
[sɔ́:sər]

n. (커피잔 등의) 받침 접시
A saucer is a small curved plate on which you stand a cup.

retire*
[ritáiər]

v. 퇴직하다, 물러나다, 은퇴하다
When older people retire, they leave their job and usually stop working completely.

wonder복습
[wʌ́ndə:r]

v. 호기심을 가지다, 이상하게 여기다; n. 경탄할 만한 것, 경이
If you wonder about something, you think about it, either because it interests you and you want to know more about it, or because you are worried or suspicious about it.

sip*
[sip]

v. 찔끔찔끔 마시다; n. 한 모금
If you sip a drink or sip at it, you drink by taking just a small amount at a time.

shortsighted
[ʃɔ:rtsàitid]

a. 근시안의, 근시안적인, 선견지명이 없는 (shortsightedly ad. 근시안적으로)
You use shortsighted to describe when someone is unable to see long-term objectives.

purse*
[pə:rs]

v. (입을) 오므리다; (눈살을) 찌푸리다; n. 지갑
If you purse your lips, you move them into a small, rounded shape, usually because you disapprove of something or when you are thinking.

snort*
[snɔ:rt]

v. 콧김을 뿜다, (경멸 등으로) 콧방귀 뀌다; n. 거센 콧김
When people or animals snort, they breathe air noisily out through their noses.

triumphant
[traiʌmfənt]

a. 의기양양한, 크게 성공한, 큰 승리를 거둔 (triumphantly ad. 의기양양하여)
Someone who is triumphant has gained a victory or succeeded in something and feels very happy about it.

blank*
[blæŋk]

a. 멍한, 얼빠진, 공허한 (blankly ad. 멍하니, 무표정하게)
If you look blank, your face shows no feeling, understanding, or interest.

reliable*
[riláiəbl]

a. 믿을 수 있는, 의지가 되는; n. 의지[신뢰]할 수 있는 사람[것]
People or things that are reliable can be trusted to work well or to behave in the way that you want them to.

specific**
[spisífik]

n. (pl.) (어떤 주제에 대한 논의 등을 위해 필요한) 세부 사항[내용];
a. 명확한, 구체적인, 특정의
The specifics of a subject are the details of it that need to be considered.

alarm*
[əlá:rm]

v. 불안하게[두렵게] 만들다; 경보장치를 달다; n. 불안, 공포; 경보(음), 경고 신호
(alarmed a. 불안해[두려워]하는)
If someone is alarmed, they feel afraid or anxious that something unpleasant or dangerous might happen.

mantelpiece
[mǽntlpì:s]

n. 벽난로 위 선반
A mantelpiece is a wood or stone shelf which is the top part of a border round a fireplace.

jar**
[dʒɑːr]

n. 병, 단지
A jar is a glass container with a lid that is used for storing food.

thimble
[θimbl]

n. 골무
A thimble is a small metal or plastic object which you use to protect your finger when you are sewing.

brass*
[bræs]

n. 놋쇠, 황동
Brass is a yellow-colored metal made from copper and zinc.

blind**
[blaind]

v. (잠시) 앞이 안보이게 만들다; 눈이 멀게하다; a. 눈먼, 장님인; 맹목적인
(blindness n. 눈에 보이지 않음; 맹목, 무지)
If something blinds you, it makes you unable to see, either for a short time or permanently.

fist*
[fist]

n. (쥔) 주먹
Your hand is referred to as your fist when you have bent your fingers in toward the palm in order to hit someone, to make an angry gesture, or to hold something.

chapter three

1. Why did Coraline and her mother go to town?
   A. They needed to buy groceries.
   B. They wanted to see a movie.
   C. They needed to buy Coraline new clothes for school.
   D. They needed to find the new school for Coraline.

2. What in particular did Coraline want to buy and why did she want it?
   A. She wanted green gloves to be unique.
   B. She wanted white socks to fit in with everybody else.
   C. She wanted a sweater to keep warm in the winter.
   D. She wanted boots shaped like frogs to play in the rain.

3. Why did Coraline's mother go back to town?
   A. She had forgotten something at the clothing store.
   B. She needed gas for her car.
   C. She wanted to go buy some food.
   D. She needed to go for her work.

4. How had the doorway changed since the first time Coraline opened it?
   A. The bricks were a different color.
   B. The door opened to a dark hallway.
   C. The door opened all by itself without Coraline's key.
   D. The key didn't work this time.

5. How was Coraline's other mother NOT different from her real mother?
   A. Her skin was lighter.
   B. She was taller and thinner.
   C. She had green eyes.
   D. Her fingers were longer and sharper.

6. How did Coraline feel about the meal her other mother made for her?
   A. She didn't want to eat it at first.
   B. She thought it was the best chicken she ever had.
   C. She was suspicious of whether or not it was poisoned.
   D. She liked her father's recipes better.

7. How did Coraline feel about the song the rats sang?
   A. She thought she had heard it before.
   B. She was bored by it.
   C. She knew the song very well.
   D. She was unbelievably happy.

1분에 몇 단어를 읽는지 리딩 속도를 측정해보세요.

$$\frac{2{,}053 \text{ words}}{\text{reading time (\quad) sec}} \times 60 = (\qquad) \text{ WPM}$$

Build Your Vocabulary

shone[*]
[ʃoun]

v. SHINE(빛나다, 비추다)의 과거 · 과거분사
Something that shines is very bright and clear because it is reflecting light.

wave^{**}
[weiv]

v. 흔들다; 물결치다; n. 흔들기; 물결, 파도
If you wave or wave your hand, you move your hand from side to side in the air, usually in order to say hello or goodbye to someone.

prefer^{**}
[prifə́:r]

vt. ~을 좋아하다, 차라리 ~을 택하다
If you prefer someone or something, you like that person or thing better than another, and so you are more likely to choose them if there is a choice.

ignore^{**}
[ignɔ́:r]

vt. 무시하다, 모르는 체하다
If you ignore someone or something, you pay no attention to them.

embarrass^{**}
[embǽrəs]

v. 당황스럽게 만들다, 곤란하게 하다
(embarrassingly ad. 당황스러울 정도로, 곤혹스럽게)
If something or someone embarrasses you, they make you feel shy or ashamed.

baggy
[bǽgi]

a. 자루 같은, 헐렁한, 불룩한
If a piece of clothing is baggy, it hangs loosely on your body.

wander^{***}
[wɑ́ndər]

v. 돌아다니다, 방황하다; n. 유랑, 방랑
If you wander in a place, you walk around there in a casual way, often without intending to go in any particular direction.

display^{***}
[displéi]

n. 진열품, 전시; v. 보이다, 나타내다, 진열(전시)하다
A display is an arrangement of things that have been put in a particular place, so that people can see them easily.

on earth

idiom (의문사를 강조하여) 도대체, 어떻게
'On earth' is often used to suggest that there is no obvious or easy answer to the question being asked.

kidnap[*]
[kídnæp]

v. 납치[유괴]하다
To kidnap someone is to take them away illegally and by force, and usually to hold them prisoner in order to demand something from their family, employer, or government.

alien[*]
[éiljən]

n. 외계인, 우주인; 외국인; a. 우주의; 외국의, 성질이 다른
In science fiction, an alien is a creature from outer space.

outer space [áutər speis]	n. (대기권 외) 우주 공간 Outer space is the area outside the earth's atmosphere where the other planets and stars are situated.
ray[*] [rei]	n. 광선, 빛; v. 번쩍이다 Rays of light are narrow beams of light.
fool[*] [fu:l]	v. 놀리다, 속이다 If someone fools you, they deceive or trick you.
wig[*] [wig]	n. 가발; 머리 장식 A wig is a covering of false hair which you wear on your head.
foreign^{**} [fɔ́:rən]	a. 외국의, 외국에서 온 Something or someone that is foreign comes from or relates to a country that is not your own.
stuff[*] [stʌf]	n. 물건, 물질; vt. 채워 넣다, 속을 채우다 You can use stuff to refer to things such as a substance, a collection of things, events, or ideas in a general way without mentioning the thing itself by name.
crust[*] [krʌst]	n. (빵) 껍질; 딱딱한 층, 표면 The crust on a loaf of bread is the outside part.
bin [bin]	n. (뚜껑 달린) 큰 상자; 쓰레기통 A bin is a container that you keep or store things in.
dash^{복습} [dæʃ]	v. 돌진하다; 내던지다; n. 돌격; 소량 If you dash somewhere, you run or go there quickly and suddenly.
suit yourself	idiom 마음대로 해라, 네 멋대로 해라 If you say 'suit yourself,' you tell somebody to do what they want, even though it annoys you.
purse^{복습} [pə:rs]	n. 지갑; v. (입을) 오므리다; (눈살을) 찌푸리다 A purse is a very small bag that people, especially women, keep their money in.
flip[*] [flip]	v. (책 등을) 휙휙 넘기다, 튕겨 올리다, 확 뒤집다; n. 손가락으로 튕김 If you flip through the pages of a book, for example, you quickly turn over the pages in order to find a particular one or to get an idea of the contents.
distant^{**} [dístənt]	a. 먼, (멀리) 떨어져 있는 Distant means very far away.
dip[*] [dip]	v. 담그다, 적시다; 가라앉다, 내려가다 If you dip something in a liquid, you put it into the liquid for a short time, so that only part of it is covered, and take it out again.
dye[*] [dai]	n. 염료, 염색제; v. 물들이다, 염색하다 Dye is a substance made from plants or chemicals which is mixed into a liquid and used to change the color of something such as cloth or hair.

ash*
[æʃ]

n. 재; 유해
Ash is the gray or black powdery substance that is left after something is burned.

particular**
[pərtíkjulər]

a. 특정한, 특별한, 특유의 (particularly ad. 특히, 두드러지게)
You use particular to emphasize that you are talking about one thing or one kind of thing rather than other similar ones.

pointless
[pɔ́intlis]

a. 무의미한, 할 가치가 없는
If you say that something is pointless, you are criticizing it because it has no sense or purpose.

broom*
[bru:m]

n. 비, 빗자루
A broom is a kind of brush with a long handle.

cupboard복습
[kʌbərd]

n. 붙박이장, 벽장, 식기장, 찬장
A cupboard is a piece of furniture that has one or two doors, usually contains shelves, and is used to store things.

chink
[tʃiŋk]

n. 쟁그랑, 땡그랑; v. 쟁그랑[땡그렁]거리다
Chink is a light and high-pitched ringing sound, as of glasses or coins striking together.

triumphant복습
[traiʌmfənt]

a. 의기양양한; 크게 성공한, 큰 승리를 거둔 (triumphantly ad. 의기양양하여)
Someone who is triumphant has gained a victory or succeeded in something and feels very happy about it.

lean복습
[li:n]

① v. ~을 기대어 세우다; 상체를 굽히다, 기울다; 의지하다 ② a. 야윈, 마른
If you lean an object on or against something, you place the object so that it is partly supported by that thing.

inherit*
[inhérit]

v. 상속하다, 물려받다, 유전하다
If you inherit money or property, you receive it from someone who has died.

ashtray
[æʃtrei]

n. (담배) 재떨이
An ashtray is a container into which people who smoke put ash, cigarette ends, etc.

work out

phrasal v. ~을 알아내다, 해결하다; 운동하다
If you work out something, you solve or find out it by reasoning.

knickknack
[níknæk]

n. 작은 물건; 자지레한 장신구; 골동품
Knickknacks are small objects which people keep as ornaments or toys, rather than for a particular use.

mantelpiece복습
[mǽntlpi:s]

n. 벽난로 위 선반
A mantelpiece is a wood or stone shelf which is the top part of a border round a fireplace.

statue*
[stǽtʃu:]

n. 상(像), 조각상
A statue is a large sculpture of a person or an animal, made of stone or metal.

smooth**
[smu:ð]

a. 매끄러운; 유창한; v. 매끄럽게 하다, 반반하게 하다
(smoothly ad. 매끄럽게, 원활히)
You use smooth to describe something that is going well and is free of problems or trouble.

32

clunk
[klʌŋk]

n. 쾅[쿵](무거운 두 물체가 부딪쳐 나는 둔탁한 소리)
A clunk is a sound made by a heavy object hitting something hard.

doorknob
[dɔ́:rnὰb]

n. 문손잡이
A doorknob is a round handle on a door.

hallway
[hɔ́:lwèi]

n. 복도; 현관
A hallway in a building is a long passage with doors into rooms on both sides of it.

musty
[mʌ́sti]

a. 곰팡이 핀, 곰팡내 나는; 케케묵은, 진부한
Something that is musty smells old and damp.

doorway^{복합}
[dɔ́:rwèi]

n. 문간, 현관, 출입구
A doorway is a space in a wall where a door opens and closes.

corridor*
[kɔ́:ridər]

n. 복도
A corridor is a long passage in a building or train, with doors and rooms on one or both sides.

unease
[ὰní:z]

n. 불안, 걱정 (uneasily ad. 불안하게, 근심이 되어)
If you have a feeling of unease, you feel rather anxious or afraid, because you think that something is wrong.

confuse*
[kənfjú:z]

v. 어리둥절하게 하다, 혼동하다 (confused a. 당황한, 어리둥절한)
To confuse someone means to make it difficult for them to know exactly what is happening or what to do.

old-fashioned*
[ould-fǽʃənd]

a. 구식의, 유행에 뒤떨어진
Something such as a style, method, or device that is old-fashioned is no longer used, done, or admired by most people, because it has been replaced by something that is more modern.

expression*
[ikspréʃən]

n. 표정, 표현, 표현법
Your expression is the way that your face looks at a particular moment. It shows what you are thinking or feeling.

nasty*
[nǽsti]

a. 심술궂은, 비열한; 더러운, 불쾌한
Something that is nasty is very unpleasant to see, experience, or feel.

indeed***
[indíd]

ad. 실로, 참으로, 과연, 정말
You use indeed to confirm or agree with something that has just been said.

peculiar*
[pikjú:ljər]

a. 기묘한, 이상한, 특이한; 특유한, 고유의
If you describe someone or something as peculiar, you think that they are strange or unusual, sometimes in an unpleasant way.

figure out

phrasal v. ~을 생각해내다, 발견하다
If you figure out a solution to a problem or the reason for something, you succeed in solving it or understanding it.

curve*
[kə:rv]

v. 구부러지다, 만곡하다; n. 곡선, 곡면 (curved a. 굽은, 곡선 모양의)
If something curves, or if someone or something curves it, it has the shape of a curve.

starve*
[staːrv]

v. 굶주리다, 굶어죽다
If people starve, they suffer greatly from lack of food which sometimes leads to their death.

roast*
[roust]

v. 굽다, 그을리다, 뜨겁게 하다 (roasted a. 구운, 볶은)
When you roast meat or other food, you cook it by dry heat in an oven or over a fire.

shovel*
[ʃʌvəl]

v. 대량으로 그러모으다(넣다); ~을 삽으로 뜨다[파다], 삽으로 일하다; n. 삽
If you shovel something somewhere, you push a lot of it quickly into that place.

proper복습
[prɑ́pər]

a. 적당[타당]한; 예의 바른; 고유의
The proper thing is the one that is correct or most suitable.

packet*
[pǽkit]

n. (상품 포상용) 통, 갑; 소포, (선물) 꾸러미
A packet is a small container in which a quantity of something is sold.

frozen*
[frouzn]

a. (식품이) 냉동된; 추워서 꽁꽁 얼 것 같은; v. FREEZE(얼다)의 과거분사형
Frozen food has been preserved by being kept at a very low temperature.

stew복습
[stjuː]

v. [약한] 불로 끓(이)다; n. 스튜 (요리)
When you stew meat, vegetables, or fruit, you cook them slowly in liquid in a closed dish.

prune
[pruːn]

① n. 서양 자두, 말린 자두; ② vt. (가지 · 뿌리 등을) 잘라내다, 치다
A prune is a dried plum.

pastry*
[péistri]

n. 가루 반죽; 빵과자
Pastry is a food made from flour, fat, and water that is mixed together, rolled flat, and baked in the oven.

principle**
[prínsəpl]

n. 원칙, 원리; 주의, 근본 방침 (on principle idiom 원칙적으로, 신념에 따라)
A principle is a general belief that you have about the way you should behave, which influences your behavior.

cautious복습
[kɔ́ːʃəs]

a. 조심성 있는, 신중한 (cautiously ad. 조심스럽게)
Someone who is cautious acts very carefully in order to avoid possible danger.

gleam*
[gliːm]

vi. 빛나다, 반짝이다, 번득이다; n. 번득임, 어스레한 빛
If an object or a surface gleams, it reflects light because it is shiny and clean.

look forward to

phrasal v. ~을 고대하다
To look forward to means to feel excited about something that is going to happen because you expect to enjoy it.

turn out

phrasal v. 결국은 ~이 되다, 결국은 ~임이 밝혀지다
To turn out means to happen in a particular way or to have a particular result.

washing up
[wɑ́ʃiŋ ʌp]

n. 설거지
To do the washing up means to wash the plates, cups, cutlery, and pans which have been used for cooking and eating a meal.

34

off-putting
[ɔ́ːf-pùtiŋ]

a. 정이 안 가는, 불쾌한
If you describe a quality or feature of something as off-putting, you mean that it makes you dislike that thing or not want to get involved with it.

shade[**]
[ʃeid]

n. 색조; (시원한) 그늘; v. 그늘지게 하다
A shade of a particular color is one of its different forms.

scheme[*]
[skiːm]

n. 계획, 설계; 음모; v. 계획하다; 음모를 꾸미다
A scheme is someone's plan for achieving something.

awful[**]
[ɔ́ːfəl]

ad. 몹시; a. 엄청, 굉장한; 몹시 나쁜, 지독한
You can use awful with noun groups that refer to an amount in order to emphasize how large that amount is.

sort[복습]
[sɔːrt]

n. 종류, 부류; vt. 분류하다, 골라내다
If you talk about a particular sort of something, you are talking about a class of things that have particular features in common.

remarkable[*]
[rimɑ́ːrkəbl]

a. 비범한, 뛰어난; 주목할 만한
Someone or something that is remarkable is unusual or special in a way that makes people notice them and be surprised or impressed.

windup
[wáindʌp]

a. 감아올리는, 태엽으로 움직이는; n. 결말, 끝장
A windup device is a mechanical device with a handle or key that you turn several times before you use it in order to make it work.

flutter[*]
[flʌtəːr]

v. (깃발 등이) 펄럭이다, (새 등이) 날갯짓하다; n. 펄럭임
If something thin or light flutters, or if you flutter it, it moves up and down or from side to side with a lot of quick, light movements.

startle[*]
[staːrtl]

v. 깜짝 놀라게 하다; 움찔하다; n. 깜짝 놀람 (startled a. 깜짝 놀란)
If something sudden and unexpected startles you, it surprises and frightens you slightly.

sparrow[**]
[spǽrou]

n. [동물] 참새
A sparrow is a small brown bird that is very common in Britain.

writhe
[raið]

v. 몸부림치다, 몸을 뒤틀다; n. 몸부림, 뒹굴기; 고뇌
If you writhe, your body twists and turns violently backward and forward, usually because you are in great pain or discomfort.

crawl[**]
[krɔːl]

vi. 기어가다, 느릿느릿 가다; n. 기어감; 서행
When you crawl, you move forward on your hands and knees.

shimmer
[ʃímər]

vi. 희미하게 반짝이다, 빛나다; n. 반짝임
If something shimmers, it shines with a faint, unsteady light or has an unclear, unsteady appearance.

skull[*]
[skʌl]

n. 두개골, 해골
Your skull is the bony part of your head which encloses your brain.

chatter[*]
[tʃǽtər]

v. (공포·추위로 이가) 딱딱 맞부딪치다; 수다를 떨다, 재잘거리다
If your teeth chatter, they keep knocking together because you are very cold or very nervous.

more like it
idiom 생각하고 있는 것에 더욱 가까운
If you say one thing is more like it, you think that is a better description of something.

horizon**
[həráizn]
n. 지평선, 수평선
The horizon is the line in the far distance where the sky seems to meet the land or the sea.

scurry
[skə́:ri]
vi. 종종걸음으로 달리다, 급히 가다
When people or small animals scurry somewhere, they move there quickly and hurriedly, especially because they are frightened.

vanish*
[vǽniʃ]
v. 사라지다, 없어지다, 모습을 감추다
If someone or something vanishes, they disappear suddenly or in a way that cannot be explained.

swift*
[swift]
a. 빠른, 신속한 (swiftly ad. 빨리, 즉시)
A swift event or process happens very quickly or without delay.

fall apart
phrasal v. 무너지다, 산산조각나다
If something falls apart, it breaks into many pieces.

scamper
[skǽmpər]
vi. 재빨리 달리다, 날쌔게 움직이다
When people or small animals scamper somewhere, they move there quickly with small, light steps.

burrow*
[bə́:rou]
v. 파고 들다; 굴을 파다, 굴에 살다[숨다]; n. 굴, 은신처
If an animal burrows into the ground or into a surface, it moves through it by making a tunnel or hole.

trouser
[tráuzə:r]
n. (pl.) 바지
Trousers are a piece of clothing that you wear over your body from the waist downward, and that cover each leg separately.

swing복습
[swiŋ]
v. (swung–swung) 흔들다, 휘두르다; 휙 돌리다, 회전시키다, 빙 돌다; 매달리다
If something swings or if you swing it, it moves repeatedly backward and forward or from side to side from a fixed point.

evidence*
[évədəns]
n. 증거, 흔적; vt. 증명하다
Evidence is anything that you see, experience, read, or are told that causes you to believe that something is true or has really happened.

restless*
[réstlis]
a. 항상 움직이는, 가만히 못 있는; 침착하지 못한, 불안한
If someone is restless, they keep moving around because they find it difficult to keep still.

lump*
[lʌmp]
n. 덩어리, 한 조각; v. 한 덩어리로 만들다
A lump of something is a solid piece of it.

slide복습
[slaid]
v. 미끄러지다, 미끄러지듯 움직이다
If you slide somewhere, you move there smoothly and quietly.

glitter*
[glítər]
vi. 반짝반짝 빛나다, 반짝이다; n. 반짝거림, 광채
If something glitters, light comes from or is reflected off different parts of it.

36

nod **

[nad]

v. 끄덕이다, 끄덕여 표시하다; n. (동의 · 인사 · 신호 · 명령의) 끄덕임

If you nod, you move your head downward and upward to show agreement, understanding, or approval.

identical *

[aidéntikəl]

a. 동일한, 꼭 같은

Things that are identical are exactly the same.

chapter four

1. What part of the other house outside is especially different from the real house?
   A. The door to Coraline's flat.
   B. The door around Miss Spink and Miss Forcible's flat.
   C. The garden around the house.
   D. The door to the old man's flat.

2. When Coraline is talking with the cat, half of her wanted to be very rude to it, but the other half wanted to be

   _____.

   A. quiet and cheerful
   B. polite and deferential
   C. annoyed and angry
   D. loud and excited

3. How did the cat say it got to the place?
   A. It followed Miss Spink through the door.
   B. It was let in by the other mother.
   C. It walked and found its own way.
   D. It was created in the other world.

4. What did Coraline volunteer to do for the other Miss Spink and Miss Forcible?

   A. She had a dagger thrown at a balloon above her head.

   B. She walked their dogs for them.

   C. She threw a dagger at them on stage.

   D. She sang a song on stage.

5. In order to stay, what did the other parents imply that Coraline needed to do?

   A. She needed to bring a special key to them.

   B. She needed to sew black buttons over her eyes.

   C. She needed to find something for them.

   D. She needed to cook a dinner for them.

6. Why did Coraline feel frightened on her way back home?

   A. She wasn't sure if the doorway would be open again.

   B. She didn't want to say goodbye to the other mother and father.

   C. She was afraid of the dark.

   D. She felt like there was something in the dark with her.

Check Your Reading Speed

1분에 몇 단어를 읽는지 리딩 속도를 측정해보세요.

$$\frac{2{,}483 \text{ words}}{\text{reading time ( ) sec}} \times 60 = (\quad\quad) \text{ WPM}$$

Build Your Vocabulary

lightbulb
[láitbʌlb]

n. 백열전구
A lightbulb is the round glass part of an electric light or lamp which light shines from.

spell[**]
[spel]

v. 철자를 말하다, (낱말을) 맞춤법에 따라 쓰다; n. 주문(呪文), 주술; 마력, 마법
When you spell a word, you write or speak each letter in the word in the correct order.

chase[**]
[tʃeis]

v. 뒤쫓다; 쫓아내다; 추구하다; n. 추적, 추격
If you chase someone, or chase after them, you run after them or follow them quickly in order to catch or reach them.

astound
[əstáund]

vt. 몹시 놀라게 하다, 망연자실하게 하다 (astounding a. 놀라운, 간담이 서늘한)
If something astounds you, you are very surprised by it.

theatrical[*]
[θiǽtrikəl]

n. 연극 공연; a. 연극[공연]의; 과장된
Theatrical is a performance of a play.

triumph[*]
[tráiəmf]

n. 승리감, 환희; 승리, 대성공; vi. 성공하다, 이기다
Triumph is a feeling of great satisfaction and pride resulting from a success or victory.

identical[복습]
[aidéntikəl]

a. 동일한, 꼭 같은
Things that are identical are exactly the same.

tip[*]
[tip]

① v. 기울이다; 뒤집(히)다 ② n. (뾰족한) 끝 ③ n. 팁, 사례금
If you tip an object or part of your body or if it tips, it moves into a sloping position with one end or side higher than the other.

glint
[glint]

v. 반짝이다, 빛나다; n. 반짝임, 섬광
If something glints, it produces or reflects a quick flash of light.

spread[***]
[spred]

v. (spread–spread) 퍼지다, 펴다, 펼치다; 뿌리다; n. 퍼짐, 폭, 넓이
If something spreads or is spread by people, it gradually reaches or affects a larger and larger area or more and more people.

shrug[복습]
[ʃrʌg]

v. (양 손바닥을 내보이면서 어깨를) 으쓱하다; n. 으쓱하기
If you shrug, you raise your shoulders to show that you are not interested in something or that you do not know or care about something.

smooth[복습]
[smuːð]

a. 부드러운, 매끄러운; 유창한; v. 매끄럽게 하다, 반반하게 하다
A smooth line or movement has no sudden breaks or changes in direction or speed.

40

whisker^{복습}
[wískə:r]

n. (고양이 · 쥐 등의) 수염; 구레나룻
The whiskers of an animal such as a cat or a mouse are the long stiff hairs that grow near its mouth.

leap[*]
[li:p]

v. (leapt/leaped–leapt/leaped) 껑충 뛰다, 뛰어넘다; n. 뜀, 도약
If you leap, you jump high in the air or jump a long distance.

expert[*]
[ékspə:rt]

n. 전문가; a. 숙련된, 노련한
An expert is a person who is very skilled at doing something or who knows a lot about a particular subject.

apparent[*]
[əpǽrənt]

a. 또렷한, 명백한; 외관상의 (apparently ad. 보아하니, 명백히)
If something is apparent to you, it is clear and obvious to you.

unaware[*]
[ʌnəwéər]

a. 알지 못하는
If you are unaware of something, you do not know about it.

existence^{**}
[igzístəns]

n. 존재, 생존
The existence of something is the fact that it is present in the world as a real thing.

rare^{**}
[rɛər]

a. 드문, 진귀한
An event or situation that is rare does not occur very often.

specimen[*]
[spésəmən]

n. 견본, 표본
A specimen is a single plant or animal which is an example of a particular species or type and is examined by scientists.

exotic
[igzátik]

a. 외래의, 외국의, 이국풍의
Something that is exotic is unusual and interesting, usually because it comes from a distant country.

breed[*]
[bri:d]

n. 품종, 유형; v. 낳다; 양육하다, 기르다
A breed of a pet animal or farm animal is a particular type of it. For example, terriers are a breed of dog.

catty
[kǽti]

a. 심술궂게 말 하는 (cattily ad. 심술궂게; 고양이같이)
If someone, especially a woman or girl, is being catty, they are being unpleasant and unkind.

dart[*]
[da:rt]

v. (시선 · 화살 · 빛 등을) 던지다, 쏘다; n. 던지는 화살, 다트
If you dart a look at someone or something, or if your eyes dart to them, you look at them very quickly.

yawn[*]
[jɔ:n]

vi. 하품하다; n. 하품
If you yawn, you open your mouth very wide and breathe in more air than usual, often when you are tired or when you are not interested in something.

reveal[*]
[riví:l]

vt. 드러내다, 보이다, 나타내다
If you reveal something that has been out of sight, you uncover it so that people can see it.

irritate[*]
[írətèit]

vt. 짜증나게 하다, 화나게 하다 (irritatingly ad. 짜증나게, 귀찮게)
If something irritates you, it keeps annoying you.

self-centered
[self-séntərd]

a. 자기 중심의, 이기적인; 자주적인, 독립한
If you have self-centered mind, you are limited to or caring only about yourself and your own needs.

deferential
[dèfərénʃəl]

a. 경의를 표하는, 공손한
Someone who is deferential is polite and respectful toward someone else.

glance*
[glæns]

v. 흘긋 보다, 잠깐 보다; **n.** 흘긋 봄
If you glance at something or someone, you look at them very quickly and then look away again immediately.

lawn*
[lɔːn]

n. 잔디밭, 잔디
A lawn is an area of grass that is kept cut short and is usually part of someone's garden or backyard, or part of a park.

by the by

idiom 그건 그렇고
You use 'by the by' when you introduce a new topic.

sensible**
[sénsəbl]

a. 상식적인, 분별 있는; 느낄 수 있는
Sensible actions or decisions are good because they are based on reasons rather than emotions.

protect 복습
[prətékt]

v. 보호하다, 막다, 지키다 (protection **n.** 보호, 방어; 방어물)
To protect someone or something means to prevent them from being harmed or damaged.

hang on

phrasal v. 꽉 붙잡다, 단단히 매달리다; **idiom** 잠깐 기다리세요
If you hang on to something, you cling, grasp, or hold it.

pause 복습
[pɔːz]

vi. 잠시 멈추다, 중단하다; **n.** 멈춤, 중지
If you pause while you are doing something, you stop for a short period and then continue.

intent*
[intént]

① **a.** 집중된, 열심인, 여념이 없는 ② **n.** 의지, 의향 (intently **ad.** 골똘하게)
If you are intent on doing something, you are eager and determined to do it.

crouch*
[krautʃ]

n. 웅크림; **v.** 몸을 쭈그리다, 쪼그리고 앉다; 웅크리다
If you are crouching, your legs are bent under you so that you are close to the ground and leaning forward slightly.

stalk*
[stɔːk]

① **vi.** 살그머니 다가가다, 몰래 접근하다; 활보하다, 으스대며 걷다
② **n.** 줄기, 잎자루
If you stalk a person or a wild animal, you follow them quietly in order to kill them, catch them, or observe them carefully.

invisible*
[invízəbl]

a. 보이지 않는, 볼 수 없는
If you describe something as invisible, you mean that it cannot be seen, for example because it is transparent, hidden, or very small.

abrupt*
[əbrápt]

a. 갑작스러운, 뜻밖의; 퉁명스러운 (abruptly **ad.** 갑자기)
An abrupt change or action is very sudden, often in a way which is unpleasant.

dash 복습
[dæʃ]

v. 돌진하다; 내던지다; **n.** 돌격; 소량
If you dash somewhere, you run or go there quickly and suddenly.

vanish^{복습}
[vǽniʃ]

v. 사라지다, 없어지다, 모습을 감추다
If someone or something vanishes, they disappear suddenly or in a way that cannot be explained.

wonder^{복습}
[wʌ́ndə:r]

v. 호기심을 가지다, 이상하게 여기다; n. 경탄할 만한 것, 경이
If you wonder about something, you think about it, either because it interests you and you want to know more about it, or because you are worried or suspicious about it.

edge^{복습}
[edʒ]

v. 조금씩[살살] 움직이다[이동시키다]; 테두리를 두르다; n. 가장자리, 변두리, 끝
If someone or something edges somewhere, they move very slowly in that direction.

bare***
[bɛər]

a. 텅 빈; 벌거벗은; 있는 그대로의; v. 드러내다
If a room, cupboard, or shelf is bare, it is empty.

dim*
[dim]

a. 희미한, 어둑한, 흐릿한; v. 어둑하게 하다, 흐려지다
Dim light is not bright.

spotlight*
[spátlàit]

n. 스포트라이트, 집중 광선; (세상의) 주시, 주목
A spotlight is a powerful light, for example in a theater, which can be directed so that it lights up a small area.

row*
[rou]

① n. 열, 줄; 좌석 줄 ② vi. (노를 써서) 배를 젓다; (배가) 저어지다
A row of things or people is a number of them arranged in a line.

shuffle*
[ʃʌfl]

v. 질질 끌다, 발을 끌며 걷다; 카드를 뒤섞다; n. 발을 끌며 걷기; 뒤섞기
If you shuffle somewhere, you walk there without lifting your feet properly off the ground.

muzzle
[mʌzl]

n. (동물의) 주둥이, 부리; 총구, 포구; vt. 재갈 물리다, 말 못하게 하다
The muzzle of an animal such as a dog is its nose and mouth.

gruff
[grʌf]

a. (목소리가) 거친, 쉰; 퉁명스러운 (gruffly ad. 거칠게; 퉁명스럽게)
A gruff voice sounds low and rough.

admit^{복습}
[ədmít]

v. 인정하다
If you admit that something bad, unpleasant, or embarrassing is true, you agree, often unwillingly, that it is true.

gloomy*
[glú:mi]

a. 우울한, 침울한; 어둑어둑한 (gloomily ad. 침울하게)
If people are gloomy, they are unhappy and have no hope.

bold*
[bould]

a. 대담한, 용감한; 뻔뻔스러운; (선 등이) 굵은
Someone who is bold is not afraid to do things which involve risk or danger.

trot*
[trat]

v. 빠른 걸음으로 가다; 총총걸음 치다; n. 빠른 걸음
If you trot somewhere, you move fairly fast at a speed between walking and running, taking small quick step.

shone^{복습}
[ʃoun]

v. SHINE(빛나다, 비추다)의 과거 · 과거분사
Something that shines is very bright and clear because it is reflecting light.

wander^{복습}
[wándər]

v. 돌아다니다, 방황하다; n. 유랑, 방랑
If you wander in a place, you walk around there in a casual way, often without intending to go in any particular direction.

inhabitant *
[inhǽbətənt]

n. 주민, 거주자
The inhabitants of a place are the people who live there.

hiss *
[his]

v. 쉿 하는 소리를 내다; n. 쉿 (제지 · 힐책의 소리)
To hiss means to make a sound like a long 's'.

scratch *
[skrætʃ]

v. 긁다, 할퀴다; n. 할큄, 찰과상 (scratchy a. (펜 따위가) 긁히는 소리를 내는)
If you scratch yourself, you rub your fingernails against your skin because it is itching.

juggle
[dʒʌgl]

v. 저글링(공 세개를 공중에서 돌리는 묘기)을 하다; 마술을 하다; 속이다;
n. 요술, 사기
If you juggle, you entertain people by throwing things into the air, catching each one and throwing it up again so that there are several of them in the air at the same time.

skip *
[skip]

v. 뛰어다니다, 깡충깡충 뛰다; 건너뛰다, 생략하다
If you skip along, you move almost as if you are dancing, with a series of little jumps from one foot to the other.

scatter **
[skǽtər]

v. 흩뿌리다, 뿌리다; 뿔뿔이 흩어지다
If you scatter things over an area, you throw or drop them so that they spread all over the area.

petal
[pétəl]

n. 꽃잎
The petals of a flower are the thin colored or white parts which together form the flower.

nimble
[nimbl]

a. 재빠른, 민첩한; 영리한 (nimbly ad. 민첩하게, 재빠르게)
Someone who is nimble is able to move their fingers, hands, or legs quickly and easily.

thump *
[θʌmp]

v. 부딪치다, 세게 때리다; n. 탁[쿵] 하는 소리; 때림, 세게 쥐어박음
If you thump something somewhere or if it thumps there, it makes a loud, dull sound by hitting something else.

bark *
[baːrk]

① v. 짖다; 고함치다, 소리 지르며 말하다 ② n. 나무 껍질
When a dog barks, it makes a short, loud noise, once or several times.

enthusiastic *
[inθùːziǽstik]

a. 열렬한, 열광적인 (enthusiastically a. 열광적으로, 열중하여)
If you are enthusiastic about something, you show how much you like or enjoy it by the way that you behave and talk.

clap *
[klæp]

v. 박수를 치다; 가볍게 치다[두드리다]
When you clap, you hit your hands together to show appreciation or attract attention.

unbutton
[ʌnbʌtən]

v. (~의) 단추를 풀다[끄르다]; (마음 속을) 털어놓다
If you unbutton an item of clothing, you undo the buttons fastening it.

fluffy ᵇᵏˢ
[flʌfi]

a. 푹신한, 보풀의, 솜털의
If you describe something such as a towel or a toy animal as fluffy, you mean that it is very soft.

shell **
[ʃel]

n. 껍데기; 조가비; v. 껍데기를 벗기다
The shell of a nut or egg is the hard covering which surrounds it.

44

pale**
[peil]

a. 창백한; 엷은, 연한; 희미한; v. 엷어지(게 하)다
If someone looks pale, their face looks a lighter color than usual, usually because they are ill, frightened, or shocked.

press**
[pres]

v. 누르다, 밀어 누르다; 강요하다; n. 언론, 출판물; 누름, 압박
If you press something somewhere, you push it firmly against something else.

squeal
[skwi:l]

v. 깩깩거리다, 비명을 지르다; n. 꽥꽥거리는 소리
If someone or something squeals, they make a long, high-pitched sound.

needle**
[ni:dl]

n. 바늘, 침
A needle is a thin hollow metal rod with a sharp point.

dig**
[dig]

v. (dug–dug) 파다, 파헤치다; 찌르다; 탐구하다; n. 파기
If you dig one thing into another or if one thing digs into another, the first thing is pushed hard into the second, or presses hard into it.

whisper⁻ᵇᵃ
[hwíspə:r]

v. 속삭이다
When you whisper, you say something very quietly.

dagger
[dǽgər]

n. 단도, 단검
A dagger is a weapon like a knife with two sharp edges.

curtsy
[kə́:rtsi]

vi. (왼발을 빼고 무릎을 굽혀 몸을 약간 숙여) 절하다; n. 절, 인사
If a woman or a girl curtsies, she lowers her body briefly, bending her knees and sometimes holding her skirt with both hands, as a way of showing respect for an important person.

applaud*
[əplɔ́:d]

v. 박수를 보내다, 성원하다
When a group of people applaud, they clap their hands in order to show approval, for example when they have enjoyed a play or concert.

slap*
[slæp]

v. 찰싹 때리다; 털썩[탁] 놓다; n. 찰싹 (때림)
If you slap someone, you hit them with the palm of your hand.

thigh*
[θai]

n. 넓적다리, 허벅다리
Your thighs are the top parts of your legs, between your knees and your hips.

woof⁻ᵇᵃ
[wu:f]

vi. 날카로운(새된) 소리를 내다, 비명을 지르다; n. 날카로운 소리, 비명
If a dog woofs, it makes a low gruff sound.

addendum
[ədéndəm]

n. (특히 책의) 부록, 추가물
An addendum is an additional section at the end of a book or document.

exposition
[èkspəzíʃən]

n. 전시(회), 진열; 설명, 해설
An exposition is an exhibition in which something such as goods or works of art are shown to the public.

volunteer*
[vàləntíər]

n. 지원자; v. 자진하다, 자발적으로 나서다
A volunteer is someone who offers to do a particular task or job without being forced to do it.

chapter four

nudge
[nʌdʒ]

vt. (주의를 끌기 위해 팔꿈치로) 슬쩍 찌르다; (물건을) 조금씩[슬쩍] 움직이다
If you nudge someone, you push them gently, usually with your elbow, in order to draw their attention to something.

blindfold
[bláindfòuld]

v. 눈을 가리다; 속이다; n. 눈가리개; 눈 속임수
If you blindfold someone, you tie a strip of cloth over their eyes so that they cannot see.

squeeze*
[skwi:z]

vt. 꽉 쥐다, 짜다, 압착하다; 쑤셔 넣다; n. 압착, 짜냄
If you squeeze something, you press it firmly, usually with your hands.

fist^{복습}
[fist]

n. (쥔) 주먹
Your hand is referred to as your fist when you have bent your fingers in toward the palm in order to hit someone, to make an angry gesture, or to hold something.

pop*
[pap]

v. 뻥 하고 터지다; 불쑥 움직이다; (물건을) 쏙 넣다; n. 뻥[탁] 하는 소리; 발포
If something pops, it makes a short sharp sound.

stick
[stik]

① v. (stuck–stuck) 꽂히다, 박히다; 찔러 넣다, 찌르다; 붙이다, 달라붙다
② n. 막대기, 지팡이
If you stick a pointed object in something, or if it sticks in something, it goes into it or through it by making a cut or hole.

twang
[twæŋ]

v. 팅[윙] 하고 퉁기다[울리다]; n. 콧소리; (현악기 · 활시위 등의) 윙 하는 소리
If you twang something such as a tight string or elastic band, or if it twangs, it makes a fairly loud, ringing sound because it has been pulled and then released.

club**
[klʌb]

n. 곤봉, (골프, 하키 등의) 클럽; 클럽[구단], 사교단체
A club is a thick heavy stick that can be used as a weapon.

longing*
[lɔ́:ŋiŋ]

a. 갈망하는, 동경하는; n. 갈망, 열망 (longingly ad. 간절히)
If you feel longing or a longing for something, you have a rather sad feeling because you want it very much.

drool
[dru:l]

v. 군침을 흘리다, 침이 나오다; n. 군침
If a person or animal drools, saliva drops slowly from their mouth.

experiment**
[ikspérəmənt]

n. 실험; vi. 실험하다 (experimental a. 실험의, 실험적인)
An experiment is a scientific test which is done in order to discover what happens to something in particular conditions.

bite
[bait]

n. 한 입(의 분량); 물기; v. 물다, 물어뜯다
A bite is the amount of food you take into your mouth when you bite it.

daylight*
[déilàit]

n. 일광, 빛; 낮
Daylight is the natural light that there is during the day, before it gets dark.

stroke*
[strouk]

① vt. 쓰다듬다, 어루만지다; n. 쓰다듬기, 달램 ② n. 타격, 일격, 치기
If you stroke someone or something, you move your hand slowly and gently over them.

46

spool
[spu:l]

n. 실감개, 실패; v. 실패에 감다
A spool is a round object onto which thread, tape, or film can be wound, especially before it is put into a machine.

cotton**
[katn]

n. 무명(실); 목화, 솜; a. 면의, 무명의
Cotton is thread that is used for sewing, especially thread that is made from cotton.

grown-up*
[groun-ʌp]

n. 성인, 어른
A grown-up is an adult, used by or to children.

drift*
[drift]

v. 표류하다, 떠돌다; n. 표류; 경향, 추세
When something drifts somewhere, it is carried there by the movement of wind or water.

scuttle^{복습}
[skʌtl]

vi. 급히 가다, 황급히 달리다; 허둥지둥 도망가다
When people or small animals scuttle somewhere, they run there with short quick steps.

hesitate***
[hézətèit]

v. 주저하다, 머뭇거리다, 망설이다
If you hesitate, you do not speak or act for a short time, usually because you are uncertain, embarrassed, or worried about what you are going to say or do.

beckon
[békən]

v. 손짓[고갯짓 · 몸짓]으로 부르다, 신호하다
If you beckon to someone, you signal to them to come to you.

mouth***
[mauθ]

v. 입을 실룩거리다; 입에 넣다[먹다]; n. 입, 입구
If you mouth something, you form words with your lips without making any sound.

howl*
[haul]

v. (바람 등이) 윙윙거리다; 짖다, 울부짖다; n. 울부짖는 소리
When the wind howls, it blows hard and makes a loud noise.

beat**
[bi:t]

v. (beat–beaten/beat) (심장이) 고동치다; 치다, 두드리다; (날개를) 퍼덕거리다; n. [음악] 박자, 고동; 퍼덕임
When your heart or pulse beats, it continually makes regular rhythmic movements.

burst**
[bə:rst]

v. 터지다, 파열하다; 갑자기 ~하다; n. 폭발, 파열; 돌발
If something bursts or if you burst it, it suddenly breaks open or splits open and the air or other substance inside it comes out.

chest**
[tʃest]

n. 가슴, 흉부; (나무로 만든) 궤, 상자
Your chest is the top part of the front of your body where your ribs, lungs, and heart are.

eventually^{복습}
[ivéntʃuəli]

ad. 결국, 마침내
Eventually means at the end of a situation or process or as the final result of it.

bump**
[bʌmp]

v. (쾅 하고) 부딪치다, 충돌하다; n. 충돌; 혹
If you bump into something or someone, you accidentally hit them while you are moving.

startle^{복습}
[sta:rtl]

v. 깜짝 놀라게 하다; 움찔하다; n. 깜짝 놀람 (startled a. 깜짝 놀란)
If something sudden and unexpected startles you, it surprises and frightens you slightly.

doorway ^{복습}
[dɔ́ːrwèi]

n. 문간, 현관, 출입구
A doorway is a space in a wall where a door opens and closes.

48

chapter five

1. After Coraline locked the door, why didn't she put the keys back where they belonged?
   A. She wanted to go back to the other place very soon.
   B. She tried to put them back but couldn't reach the top of the door.
   C. She wanted her father to do it for her later.
   D. She simply didn't care about it.

2. How did Miss Spink and Miss Forcible respond to Coraline when she told them her parents were missing?
   A. They felt worried for her and offered help.
   B. They called the police for her.
   C. They ignored her and talked about their niece.
   D. They invited her in for tea again.

3. How did the cat help Coraline?
   A. It showed Coraline the mirror where she sees her parents trapped.
   B. It led her to her parent's office where they were sleeping.
   C. It brought her the keys to the doorway leading to the other place.
   D. It kept her company so that she wouldn't be afraid.

4. Why didn't the police officer help Coraline?

    A. He thought Coraline was just having a nightmare.

    B. He knew where Coraline's parents really were.

    C. He was too busy at the time.

    D. He wanted to help, but didn't know how.

5. How did the other mother try to trick Coraline into not worrying about her parents?

    A. She told Coraline that she could visit her parents anytime she wanted.

    B. She cooked Coraline another delicious meal.

    C. She told Coraline that she could see her parents after dinner.

    D. She showed her an image of her parents back from a vacation in the mirror.

6. Why did the other mother order the rat to bring back the key?

    A. She lost her own key a long time ago.

    B. She needed to give the rat something to do.

    C. There was only one key and she wanted to lock the door.

    D. She didn't want Coraline's real parents coming back through the door.

7. What kind of advice did the cat offer Coraline to help against the other mother?

    A. It suggested that Coraline challenge the other mother to a game.

    B. It suggested that Coraline run away from the other mother.

    C. It suggested that she use the stone with the hole in it to attack the other mother.

    D. It suggested that it follow her through another door out of the other world.

1분에 몇 단어를 읽는지 리딩 속도를 측정해보세요.

$$\frac{3,866 \text{ words}}{\text{reading time ( ) sec}} \times 60 = (\qquad) \text{ WPM}$$

Build Your Vocabulary

bunch*
[bʌntʃ]

n. 다발, (과일 등의) 송이; 다량; 떼, 한패
A bunch of things is a number of things, especially a large number.

accept***
[æksépt]

v. 받아들이다, 인정하다; 수락하다
If you accept an idea, statement, or fact, you believe that it is true or valid.

expedition*복습*
[ekspidiʃən]

n. 원정, (탐험 등의) 여행
An expedition is an organized journey that is made for a particular purpose such as exploration.

freezer*복습*
[fríːzər]

n. 냉동고
A freezer is a large container like a fridge in which the temperature is kept below freezing point so that you can store food inside it for long periods.

spare*
[spɛər]

a. 예비의, 여분의; n. 예비품, 비상용품; v. 아끼다, 절약하다; 할애하다
You use spare to describe something that is the same as things that you are already using, but that you do not need yet and are keeping ready in case another one is needed.

loaf*
[louf]

n. (모양을 만들어 한 덩어리로 구운) 빵 한 덩이
A loaf of bread is bread which has been shaped and baked in one piece.

compartment*
[kəmpɑ́ːrtmənt]

n. 구획, 칸막이
A compartment is one of the separate parts of an object that is used for keeping things in.

grown-up*복습*
[groun-ʌp]

n. 성인, 어른
A grown-up is an adult, used by or to children.

yawn*복습*
[jɔːn]

vi. 하품하다; n. 하품
If you yawn, you open your mouth very wide and breathe in more air than usual, often when you are tired or when you are not interested in something.

undress
[ʌndrés]

v. 옷을 벗다[벗기다]
When you undress or undress someone, you take off your clothes or someone else's clothes.

can*
[kæn]

v. 통조림하다; n. 통, 용기 (canned a. 통조림한)
When food or drink is canned, it is put into a metal container and sealed so that it will remain fresh.

52

block***
[blak]

n. 큰 덩어리; 방해(물), 장애(물); **v.** 막다, 방해하다
A block of a substance is a large rectangular piece of it.

shrivel
[ʃrívəl]

v. 쪼글쪼글해지다, 주름(살)지다, 줄어들다
When something shrivels or when something shrivels it, it becomes dryer and smaller, often with lines in its surface, as a result of losing the water it contains.

digestive
[daidʒéstiv]

a. 소화의, 소화를 돕는; **n.** 소화제
You can describe things that are related to the digestion of food as digestive.

vague*
[veig]

a. 어렴풋한, 막연한 (vaguely **ad.** 약간, 조금; 모호하게)
If you have a vague memory or idea of something, the memory or idea is not clear.

chemical*
[kémikəl]

a. 화학의, 화학으로 만든; **n.** 화학 제품[약품]
Chemical means involving or resulting from a reaction between two or more substances, or relating to the substances that something consists of.

enormous*
[inɔ́:rməs]

a. 엄청난, 거대한, 막대한 (enormously **ad.** 엄청나게, 대단히)
You can use enormous to emphasize the great degree or extent of something.

on one's own

idiom 혼자서, 자력으로
If you do something on your own, you do it without any help from other people.

press***
[pres]

n. 언론, 출판물; 누름, 압박; **v.** 누르다, 밀어 누르다; 강요하다
Newspapers are referred to as the press.

clipping
[klípiŋ]

n. (신문, 잡지의) 오려낸 기사; 가위질, 깎기
A clipping is an article, picture, or advertisement that has been cut from a newspaper or magazine.

vanish***
[væniʃ]

v. 사라지다, 없어지다, 모습을 감추다
If someone or something vanishes, they disappear suddenly or in a way that cannot be explained.

circumstance**
[sɔ́:rkəmstæns]

n. 상황, 환경, 사정
The circumstances of a particular situation are the conditions which affect what happens.

niece*
[ni:s]

n. 조카딸
Someone's niece is the daughter of their sister or brother.

glow*
[glou]

v. 빛을 내다; **n.** 빛, 밝음
If something glows, it produces a dull, steady light.

flat***
[flæt]

① **n.** (연립주택, 다세대 주택 등을 포함하는) 아파트식 주거지
② **a.** 평평한, 균일한; 단호한; **n.** 평지, 평원
A flat is a set of rooms for living in, usually on one floor and part of a larger building. A flat usually includes a kitchen and bathroom.

bat**
[bæt]

① **v.** (배트·막대기로) 치다; **n.** (야구의) 배트, 막대기 ② **n.** 박쥐
When you bat, you have a turn at hitting the ball with a bat in baseball, softball, cricket, or rounders.

indeed^{복습}
[indíd]

ad. 실로, 참으로, 과연, 정말
You use indeed to confirm or agree with something that has just been said.

corridor^{복습}
[kɔ́:ridər]

n. 복도
A corridor is a long passage in a building or train, with doors and rooms on one or both sides.

wardrobe*
[wɔ́:rdròub]

n. 옷장; 의상
A wardrobe is a tall cupboard or cabinet in which you can hang your clothes.

occasional^{복습}
[əkéiʒənl]

a. 가끔의, 때때로의 (occasionally ad. 때때로, 가끔)
Occasional means happening sometimes, but not regularly or often.

replace**
[ripléis]

v. 내신하다; 제자리에 놓다
If one thing or person replaces another, the first is used or acts instead of the second.

reflect**
[riflékt]

v. 비추다; 반사하다, 반영하다; 깊이 생각하다, 심사숙고하다
When something is reflected in a mirror or in water, you can see its image in the mirror or in the water.

awkward**
[ɔ́:kwərd]

a. 어색한, 불편한, 곤란한 (awkwardly ad. 어색하게, 거북하게)
Someone who feels awkward behaves in a shy or embarrassed way.

wave^{복습}
[weiv]

v. 흔들다; 물결치다; n. 흔들기; 물결, 파도
If you wave or wave your hand, you move your hand from side to side in the air, usually in order to say hello or goodbye to someone.

limp^{복습}
[limp]

a. 약한, 기운이 없는; 흐느적거리는
If someone is limp, their body has no strength and is not moving.

fog^{복습}
[fɔ:g]

n. 안개; 혼란
When there is fog, there are tiny drops of water in the air which form a thick cloud and make it difficult to see things.

fade*
[feid]

vi. 희미해지다; (색이) 바래다; 시들다
When a colored object fades or when the light fades it, it gradually becomes paler.

tip^{복습}
[tip]

① n. (뾰족한) 끝 ② v. 기울이다; 뒤집(히)다 ③ n. 팁, 사례금
The tip of something long and narrow is the end of it.

forefinger
[fɔ́:rfìŋgər]

n. 집게손가락
Your forefinger is the finger that is next to your thumb.

windowsill
[wíndousil]

n. 창턱, 창 아래틀
A windowsill is a shelf along the bottom of a window, either inside or outside a building.

under one's own steam

idiom 혼자 힘으로
If you go somewhere under your own steam, you get there without help from others.

gruff^{복습}
[grʌf]

a. (목소리가) 거친, 쉰; 퉁명스러운
A gruff voice sounds low and rough.

54

divert[*]
[divə́:rt]

v. (사람 · 주의를) 전환하다, 딴 데로 돌리다
If you say that someone diverts your attention from something important or serious, you disapprove of them behaving or talking in a way that stops you thinking about it.

crime[**]
[kraim]

n. 범죄, 죄
A crime is an illegal action or activity for which a person can be punished by law.

sort[복습]
[sɔ:rt]

n. 종류, 부류; vt. 분류하다, 골라내다
If you talk about a particular sort of something, you are talking about a class of things that have particular features in common.

kidnap[복습]
[kídnæ̀p]

v. 납치[유괴]하다
To kidnap someone is to take them away illegally and by force, and usually to hold them prisoner in order to demand something from their family, employer, or government.

clutch[*]
[klʌtʃ]

n. 지배(력), 수중; 움켜짐; v. 꽉 잡다, 붙들다, 부여잡다
If someone is in another person's clutches, that person has captured them or has power over them.

sew[*]
[sou]

v. 바느질하다, 꿰매다, 깁다
When you sew something such as clothes, you make them or repair them by joining pieces of cloth together by passing thread through them with a needle.

lure[*]
[luər]

vt. 유혹하다, 꾀어내다; n. 매혹물, 미끼
To lure someone means to trick them into a particular place or to trick them into doing something that they should not do.

nefarious
[niféəriəs]

a. 범죄의, 못된, 극악한
If you describe an activity as nefarious, you mean that it is wicked and immoral.

fiendish
[fí:ndiʃ]

a. 사악한, 귀신[악마] 같은; 극악의
A fiendish person enjoys being cruel.

nightmare[*]
[náitmɛər]

n. 악몽
A nightmare is a very frightening dream.

reassure[*]
[rì:əʃúər]

vt. 안심시키다 (reassuring a. 안심시키는, 위안을 주는)
If you reassure someone, you say or do things to make them stop worrying about something.

entire[*]
[intáiər]

a. 전체의; 완전한
You use entire when you want to emphasize that you are referring to the whole of something, for example, the whole of a place, time, or population.

groom
[gru:m]

vt. 단정히 가다듬다, 돌보다, 손질하다; n. 신랑
If you groom an animal, you clean its fur, usually by brushing it.

sink[***]
[siŋk]

n. (부엌의) 싱크대, 개수대; v. 가라앉다, 빠지다; 밀어넣다, 가라앉히다
A sink is a large fixed container in a kitchen, with taps to supply water. It is mainly used for washing dishes.

long since

idiom 훨씬 이전에
If you say that something has long since happened, you mean that it happened a long time ago.

run down

phrasal v. (건전지 등이) 다 되다; (기계 등이) 멈추다[정지하다]
If something like an engine, batter, etc. runs down, it loses power gradually and ceases to function.

barely*
[béərli]

ad. 간신히, 가까스로; 거의 ~않다
You use barely to say that something is only just true or only just the case.

faint*
[feint]

a. 희미한, 어렴풋한; **vi.** 기절하다
A faint sound, color, mark, feeling, or quality has very little strength or intensity.

straw*
[strɔː]

n. 짚, 밀짚; 빨대
Straw consists of the dried, yellowish stalks from crops such as wheat or barley.

in case

idiom (혹시라도) (~할) 경우에 대비해서
If you do something in case or just in case a particular thing happens, you do it because that thing might happen.

emergency**
[imə́ːrdʒənsi]

n. 비상사태, 위급함; **a.** 비상용의, 긴급한
An emergency is an unexpected and difficult or dangerous situation, especially an accident, which happens suddenly and which requires quick action to deal with it.

thrust*
[θrʌst]

v. (thrust–thrust) 밀다, 떠밀다; **n.** 추진력, 밀침, 찌름
If you thrust something or someone somewhere, you push or move them there quickly with a lot of force.

somehow**
[sʌ́mhàu]

ad. 여하튼, 어쨌든; 어쩐지, 아무래도
You use somehow to say that you do not know or cannot say how something was done or will be done.

rummage
[rʌ́midʒ]

v. 뒤지다, 샅샅이 찾다; **n.** 잡동사니; 뒤지기
If you rummage through something, you search for something you want by moving things around in a careless or hurried way.

candlewick
[kǽndlwik]

n. 양초의 심지
Candlewick is the piece of string in it which burns when it is lit.

sputter
[spʌ́tər]

v. 푸푸[지글지글, 탁탁] 소리를 내다; 흥분하여 말하다, 식식거리며 말하다
If something such as an engine or a flame sputters, it works or burns in an uneven way and makes a series of soft popping sounds.

wasteland
[wéistlæ̀nd]

n. 황무지, 불모지
A wasteland is an area of land on which not much can grow or which has been spoiled in some way.

explore복습
[eksplɔ́ər]

v. 탐험[답사] 하다, 탐구하다, 조사하다
If you explore a place, you travel around it to find out what it is like.

gully
[gʌ́li]

n. 협곡, 골짜기; 도랑, 배수구
A gully is a long narrow valley with steep sides.

urgent*
[ə́:rdʒənt]

a. 긴급한, 절박한 (urgently ad. 긴박하게)
If something is urgent, it needs to be dealt with as soon as possible.

thunder*
[θʌ́ndər]

v. 큰소리를 내(며 이동하)다; 천둥치다; n. 우레, 천둥
If something or someone thunders somewhere, they move there quickly and with a lot of noise.

charge*
[tʃɑːrdʒ]

v. 돌격하다, 돌진하다; 청구하다; 충전하다, 채우다; n. 요금; 책임
If you charge toward someone or something, you move quickly and aggressively toward them.

rhino
[rɑ́inou]

n. (= rhinoceros) 코뿔소
A rhino is a large Asian or African animal with thick gray skin and a horn, or two horns, on its nose.

sweep*
[swiːp]

v. (swept-swept) 휩쓸어 가다, 쓸다; 휙 둘러보다, 휙 지나치다;
n. 한 번 휘두름; 청소
If your arm or hand sweeps in a particular direction, or if you sweep it there, it moves quickly and smoothly in that direction.

puff*
[pʌf]

v. 숨을 헐떡거리다, (연기를) 내뿜다; 부풀어 오르다; n. 훅 불기, 숨, 입김
If you are puffing, you are breathing loudly and quickly with your mouth open because you are out of breath after a lot of physical effort.

pant*
[pænt]

vi. 헐떡거리다, 숨차다; n. 헐떡거림, 숨 가쁨
If you pant, you breathe quickly and loudly with your mouth open, because you have been doing something energetic.

rot복습
[rat]

v. 썩다, 썩이다; n. 썩음, 부패 (rotten a. 썩은)
When food, wood, or another substance rots, or when something rots it, it becomes softer and is gradually destroyed.

sting*
[stiŋ]

vt. (stung-stung) 찌르다, 쏘다; 따끔따끔하다; n. 찌름, 쏨
If something stings you, a sharp part of is pushed into your skin so that you feel a sharp pain.

whisker복습
[wískər]

n. (고양이 · 쥐 등의) 수염; 구레나룻
The whiskers of an animal such as a cat or a mouse are the long stiff hairs that grow near its mouth.

in a manner

idiom 어떤 의미로는; 어느 정도, 얼마간
You say in a manner when you think about something in a certain way.

indicate*
[índikeit]

vt. 가리키다, 지시하다, 나타내다
If one thing indicates another, the first thing shows that the second is true or exists.

impatient*
[impéiʃənt]

a. 성급한, 조급한, 참을성 없는 (impatience n. 성급함, 초조함)
If you are impatient, you are annoyed because you have to wait too long for something.

stroke복습
[strouk]

① vt. 쓰다듬다, 어루만지다; n. 쓰다듬기, 달램 ② n. 타격, 일격, 치기
If you stroke someone or something, you move your hand slowly and gently over them.

pace*
[peis]

n. 1보(의 거리), 보폭; 걸음걸이; 걷는 속도
A pace is the distance that you move when you take one step.

clunk^{복습}
[klʌŋk]

n. 쾅[쾅](무거운 두 물체가 부딪쳐 나는 둔탁한 소리)
A clunk is a sound made by a heavy object hitting something hard.

swing^{복습}
[swiŋ]

v. (swung–swung) 휙 돌리다, 회전시키다, 빙 돌다; 휘두르다, 흔들다; 매달리다
If something swings in a particular direction or if you swing it in that direction, it moves in that direction with a smooth, curving movement.

passageway
[pǽsidʒwèi]

n. 통로, 복도
A passageway is a long narrow space with walls or fences on both sides, which connects one place or room with another.

damp^{복습}
[dæmp]

a. 축축한; n. 습기
Something that is damp is slightly wet.

musty^{복습}
[mʌ́sti]

a. 곰팡이 핀, 곰팡내 나는; 케케묵은, 진부한 (mustiness n. 곰팡내, 퀴퀴한 냄새)
Something that is musty smells old and damp.

pad*
[pæd]

① v. 거닐다, 발소리를 내지 않고 걷다; ② vt. ~에 덧대다; n. 덧대는 것, 패드
When someone pads somewhere, they walk there with steps that are fairly quick, light, and quiet.

cast^{복습}
[kæst]

v. (cast–cast) (그림자 따위를) 드리우다; 내던지다; 배역을 정하다; n. 깁스, 붕대
If something casts a light or shadow somewhere, it causes it to appear there.

flicker
[flíkər]

v. (등불 · 희망 · 빛 등이) 깜박이다; n. 깜박임
If a light or flame flickers, it shines unsteadily.

fortunate**
[fɔ́:rtʃənət]

a. 운이 좋은, 행운의, 복 받은
If you say that someone is fortunate, you mean that they are lucky.

companion**
[kəmpǽnjən]

n. 길동무, 동반자; 동료, 친구
A companion is someone who you spend time with or who you are traveling with.

wisdom*
[wízdəm]

n. 지혜, 현명함
Wisdom is the ability to use your experience and knowledge in order to make sensible decisions or judgments.

intelligence**
[intélədʒəns]

n. 지능, 총명
Intelligence is the quality of being intelligent or clever.

sarcastic*
[sɑ:rkǽstik]

a. 빈정대는, 비꼬는, 풍자적인
Someone who is sarcastic says or does the opposite of what they really mean in order to mock or insult someone.

bristle
[brísl]

v. (털 등을) 곤두세우다; (화 · 용기 등을) 불러 일으키다 (bristling a. 곤두서있는)
If animal's fur bristles, it rises up as in fear.

snuff*
[snʌf]

① v. (촛불을) 끄다, 꺼지다; ② v. 코로 들이쉬다, 흥흥거리며 냄새를 맡다; n. 냄새, 향기
To snuff means to snip off the burnt part of the wick of a candle or lamp.

58

scrabble [skrǽbl]	**v.** 뒤지며[허우적거리며] 찾다; 휘갈겨 쓰다, 낙서하다; **n.** 휘갈겨 쓰기, 낙서 If you scrabble for something, especially something that you cannot see, you move your hands or your feet about quickly and hurriedly in order to find it.
patter^{복습} [pǽtər]	**v.** 후두두[타닥타닥] 하는 소리를 내다; (발걸음을) 가볍게 걸어가다; **n.** 후두두[타닥타닥] 하는 소리 If something patters on a surface, it hits the surface quickly several times, making quiet, tapping sounds.
pound* [paund]	① **v.** 쿵쿵 울리다, 마구 치다, 세게 두드리다; **n.** 타격 ② **n.** 파운드(무게의 단위) ③ **n.** 울타리, 우리 If you pound something or pound on it, you hit it with great force, usually loudly and repeatedly.
rib* [rib]	**n.** 늑골, 갈빗대; [요리] 갈비 Your ribs are the 12 pairs of curved bones that surround your chest.
wisp [wisp]	**n.** 작은 단[묶음]; 한 조각 (wispy **a.** (촘촘하지 못하고) 몇 가닥[줄기]으로 된, 성긴) A wisp of hair is a small, thin, untidy bunch of it.
blind^{복습} [blaind]	**v.** (잠시) 앞이 안보이게 만들다; 눈이 멀게하다; **a.** 눈먼, 장님인; 맹목적인 If something blinds you, it makes you unable to see, either for a short time or permanently.
silhouette [siluét]	**vt.** 실루엣으로 나타내다; ~의 그림자를 비추다; **n.** 윤곽, 실루엣 To silhouette means to represent, or make appear, as a solid dark shape.
eager*** [íːgər]	**a.** 열망하는, 간절히 하고 싶어 하는 If you are eager to do or have something, you want to do or have it very much.
relieve* [rilíːv]	**vt.** 안도하게 하다; (긴장·걱정 등을) 덜다 (relieved **a.** 안심한, 안도한) If something relieves an unpleasant feeling or situation, it makes it less unpleasant or causes it to disappear completely.
enfold [infóuld]	**v.** (다정하게) 안다, 감싸다 If you enfold someone or something, you hold them close in a very gentle, loving way.
rigid* [rídʒid]	**a.** 굳은, 단단한; 엄격한, 완고한 A rigid substance or object is stiff and does not bend, stretch, or twist easily.
tremble* [trembl]	**v.** 떨다, 떨리다 (trembling **a.** 떠는, 떨리는) If you tremble, you shake slightly because you are frightened or cold.
scarcely** [skέərsli]	**ad.** 거의 ~ 아니다, 간신히, 가까스로 You use scarcely to emphasize that something is only just true or only just the case.
reluctant* [rilʌ́ktənt]	**a.** 꺼리는, 마지못해 하는, 주저하는 (reluctance **n.** 마지못해 함) If you are reluctant to do something, you are unwilling to do it and hesitate before doing it, or do it slowly and without enthusiasm.

hallway^{복습}
[hɔ́:lwèi]

n. 복도; 현관
A hallway in a building is a long passage with doors into rooms on both sides of it.

burned-out
[bə́:rnd-áut]

a. 타버린, 못쓰게 된, 식은
If something is burned-out, it is destroyed or badly damaged by fire.

bite**
[bait]

v. (bit-bitten) 물다, 물어뜯다; n. 한 입(의 분량); 물기
If you bite something, you use your teeth to cut into it, for example in order to eat it or break it.

relish
[réliʃ]

n. 즐거움, 흥미, 의욕; 맛, 풍미; v. 즐기다; 기쁘게 생각하다
If you do something with relish, you feel pleasant.

enthusiasm*
[inθú:ziæzm]

n. 열광, 열중, 열의
Enthusiasm is great eagerness to be involved in a particular activity which you like and enjoy or which you think is important.

glitter^{복습}
[glítər]

vi. 반짝반짝 빛나다, 반짝이다; n. 반짝거림, 광채
If something glitters, light comes from or is reflected off different parts of it.

gleam^{복습}
[gli:m]

vi. 빛나다, 반짝이다, 번득이다; n. 번득임, 어스레한 빛
If an object or a surface gleams, it reflects light because it is shiny and clean.

frighten**
[fraitn]

v. 놀라게 하다, 섬뜩하게 하다; 기겁하다
If something or someone frightens you, they cause you to suddenly feel afraid, anxious, or nervous.

shimmer^{복습}
[ʃímər]

vi. 희미하게 반짝이다, 빛나다; n. 반짝임
If something shimmers, it shines with a faint, unsteady light or has an unclear, unsteady appearance.

abandon*
[əbǽndən]

vt. 버리다; 단념하다, 그만두다
If you abandon a place, thing, or person, you leave the place, thing, or person permanently or for a long time.

drift^{복습}
[drift]

v. 표류하다, 떠돌다; n. 표류; 경향, 추세
When something drifts somewhere, it is carried there by the movement of wind or water.

glare*
[glɛər]

v. 노려보다; 번쩍번쩍 빛나다; n. 섬광; 노려봄
If you glare at someone, you look at them with an angry expression on your face.

surface**
[sə́:rfis]

n. 표면, 외관; a. 표면의
The surface of something is the flat top part of it or the outside of it.

prevent**
[privént]

v. 방해하여 ~하지 못하게 하다; 막다, 방해하다
To prevent someone from doing something means to make it impossible for them to do it.

doubt***
[daut]

n. 의심; 회의; v. 의심하다, 의혹을 품다
If you have doubt or doubts about something, you feel uncertain about it and do not know whether it is true or possible.

60

core*
[kɔ:r]

n. (배 · 사과 등의) 응어리, 과심; (사물의) 핵심
The core of a fruit is the central part of it.

expression^{복습}
[ikspréʃən]

n. 표정, 표현, 표현법
Your expression is the way that your face looks at a particular moment. It shows what you are thinking or feeling.

lightning*
[láitniŋ]

n. 번개, 번갯불; a. 번개 같은,; 매우 빠른
Lightning is the very bright flashes of light in the sky that happen during thunderstorms.

illusion*
[ilú:ʒən]

n. 환영, 환각, 착각
An illusion is something that appears to exist or be a particular thing but does not actually exist or is in reality something else.

clap^{복습}
[klæp]

v. 박수를 치다; 가볍게 치다[두드리다]
When you clap, you hit your hands together to show appreciation or attract attention.

rustle*
[rʌsl]

vi. 바스락거리다, 살랑살랑 소리 내다; n. 바스락거리는 소리
(rustling a. 와삭와삭[바스락바스락] 소리 나는)
If things such as paper or leaves rustle, or if you rustle them, they move about and make a soft, dry sound.

chitter
[tʃítər]

v. 지저귀다; (추워서) 떨다
To chitter means to twitter or chirp.

drag*
[dræg]

v. 끌다, 힘들게 움직이다; n. 견인, 끌기
If you drag something, you pull it along the ground.

hush*
[hʌʃ]

int. 쉿, 조용히 해; v. 침묵하다; 잠잠하게 하다; n. 침묵, 고요함
You say 'Hush!' to someone when you are asking or telling them to be quiet.

triviality
[trìviǽləti]

n. 사소한 문제, 사소함
If you refer to something as a triviality, you think that it is unimportant and not serious.

stiff**
[stif]

a. 단단한, 뻣뻣한; 완강한, 완고한
Something that is stiff is firm or does not bend easily.

luminous
[lú:mənəs]

a. 어둠에서 빛나는, 야광의, 빛을 발하는
Something that is luminous shines or glows in the dark.

tug^{복습}
[tʌg]

v. (세게) 당기다, 끌다; 노력[분투]하다; n. 힘껏 당김; 분투, 노력
If you tug something or tug at it, you give it a quick and usually strong pull.

furry
[fɔ́:ri]

a. 털로 덮인, 부드러운 털의
If you describe something as furry, you mean that it has a soft rough texture like fur.

insinuate
[insínjuèit]

vt. 넌지시 비치다, 둘러서 말하다, 빗대어 말하다
(insinuating a. 암시하는, 의미있는 듯한)
If you say that someone insinuates that something bad is the case, you mean that they say it in an indirect way.

relief[**] [riːf]

n. 안심, 안도
If you feel a sense of relief, you feel happy because something unpleasant has not happened or is no longer happening.

recognize[**] [rékəgnàiz]

vt. 인지하다, 알아보다
If you recognize someone or something, you know who that person is or what that thing is.

wrinkle[*] [riŋkl]

v. ~에 주름살지게 하다, 구겨지다; n. 주름, 잔주름
When you wrinkle your nose or forehead, or when it wrinkles, you tighten the muscles in your face so that the skin folds.

impress[*] [imprés]

v. ~에게 (깊은) 인상을 주다; 감동시키다
(unimpressed a. 감명받지 않은, 대단하다고 생각하지 않는)
If something impresses you, you feel great admiration for it.

confide[*] [kənfáid]

v. (비밀을) 털어놓다
If you confide in someone, you tell them a secret.

overrate [òuvərréit]

v. 과대 평가하다, 너무 높게 예상하다 (overrated a. 과대 평가된)
If you say that something or someone is overrated, you mean that people have a higher opinion of them than they deserve.

might as well

idiom ~하는 편이 낫다
If you say that you might as well do something, or that you may as well do it, you mean that you will do it although you do not have a strong desire to do it and may even feel slightly unwilling to do it.

whirlwind [hwə́ːrlwìnd]

n. 회오리바람
A whirlwind is a tall column of air which spins round and round very fast and moves across the land or sea.

flick [flik]

v. 가볍게 치다, 튀기다; n. 가볍게 치기, 튀기기
If something flicks in a particular direction, or if someone flicks it, it moves with a short, sudden movement.

challenge[**] [tʃǽlindʒ]

v. 도전하다; n. 도전
If you challenge someone, you invite them to fight or compete with you in some way.

guarantee[*] [gæ̀rəntíː]

n. 보증, 개런티; vt. 보증하다, 다짐하다
Something that is a guarantee of something else makes it certain that it will happen or that it is true.

luxuriant [lʌgʒúəriənt]

a. 풍부한, 번성한, 울창한 (luxuriantly ad. 편안하게, 느긋이)
Luxuriant plants, trees, and gardens are large, healthy, and growing well.

creep[복습] [kriːp]

vi. (crept–crept) 천천히[살금살금] 걷다, 기다; n. 포복
If something creeps somewhere, it moves very slowly.

precise[*] [prisáis]

a. 정확한, 정밀한; 명확한 (precisely ad. 정밀하게, 정확히)
You use precise to emphasize that you are referring to an exact thing, rather than something vague.

62

parody
[pǽrədi]

n. 패러디(다른 것을 풍자적으로 모방한 글 · 음악 · 연극 등); (형편없는) 놀림감;
v. 패러디하다
When you say that something is a parody of a particular thing, you are criticizing it because you think it is a very poor example or bad imitation of that thing.

haul*
[hɔːl]

v. 잡아끌다, 끌어당기다; 운반하다; 체포하다
If you haul something which is heavy or difficult to move, you move it using a lot of effort.

dislodge
[dislɑ́dʒ]

v. 제거하다, 몰아내다; 철수하다; 숙소에서 나오다
To dislodge something means to remove it from where it was fixed or held.

stir*
[stəːr]

v. 움직이다; 휘젓다; n. 움직임; 휘젓기
If you stir, you move slightly, for example because you are uncomfortable or beginning to wake up.

mutter^{복습}
[mʌtər]

v. 중얼거리다, 불평하다; n. 중얼거림, 불평
If you mutter, you speak very quietly so that you cannot easily be heard, often because you are complaining about something.

chapter six

1. How did Coraline feel when she woke up?
   A. She felt relaxed.
   B. She felt very dislocated.
   C. She felt afraid of her parents.
   D. She felt very hungry.

2. What did the other father say that the other mother was out doing?
   A. He said she was out buying groceries.
   B. He said she went to Caroline's world through the doorway.
   C. He said she was out fixing the doors.
   D. He said she was trying to capture the rats.

3. Why did the other father feel nervous about talking to Coraline?
   A. He was busy with his work and couldn't pay attention.
   B. He shouldn't have been talking to Coraline when the other mother is away.
   C. He was shy around Coraline, because he didn't know her very well.
   D. He was busy trying to fix the vermin problem in the house.

4. What was different about the drawing room in the other world?

    A. There was a snow globe on the mantelpiece.

    B. There was an empty fireplace.

    C. There was a painting of fruit on the wall.

    D. There was a wooden table

5. Why was the cat unimpressed with the other mother's attempts to keep it out?

    A. It thought there were ways in and out that even she didn't know about.

    B. It had the key to all of the doors in the world.

    C. It didn't ever want to leave the world.

    D. It was friends with the rats who helped it come and go.

6. Why did the other mother send Coraline into the darkness?

    A. She wanted Coraline to eat the blackbeetles she offered.

    B. She wanted Coraline to go to sleep quietly.

    C. She wanted Coraline to meet rats.

    D. She wanted Coraline to learn some manners.

1분에 몇 단어를 읽는지 리딩 속도를 측정해보세요.

$$\frac{2,695 \text{ words}}{\text{reading time (\quad) sec}} \times 60 = (\qquad) \text{ WPM}$$

Build Your Vocabulary

utter* [ʌ́tər]	① a. 완전한, 전적인, 절대적인 ② v. 발언하다, 입을 열다 (utterly ad. 완전히) You use utter to emphasize that something is great in extent, degree, or amount.
dislocate [dísloukèit]	v. (시스템·계획 등을) 혼란에 빠뜨리다; (뼈를) 탈구시키다 (dislocated a. 혼란스러운) To dislocate something such as a system, process, or way of life means to disturb it greatly or prevent it from continuing as normal.
entire^{복습} [intáiər]	a. 전체의; 완전한 (entirely ad. 완전히, 전적으로) You use entire when you want to emphasize that you are referring to the whole of something, for example, the whole of a place, time, or population.
astonish* [əstɑ́niʃ]	vt. 깜짝 놀라게 하다 (astonishing a. 놀라운, 깜짝 놀랄 만한) If something or someone astonishes you, they surprise you very much.
fragile* [frǽdʒəl]	a. 부서지기[깨지기] 쉬운 Something that is fragile is easily broken or damaged.
daydream* [déidrì:m]	n. (즐거운 일에 관한) 백일몽, 공상 A daydream is a series of pleasant thoughts, usually about things that you would like to happen.
tap^{복습} [tæp]	① v. 가볍게 두드리다; n. 가볍게 두드리기 ② n. 주둥이, (수도 등의) 꼭지 If you tap something, you hit it with a quick light blow or a series of quick light blows.
fraction* [frǽkʃən]	n. 파편, 단편; 조금, 소량; [수학] 분수 A fraction of something is a tiny amount or proportion of it.
rustle^{복습} [rʌsl]	vi. 바스락거리다, 살랑살랑 소리 내다; n. 바스락거리는 소리 (rustling a. 와삭와삭[바스락바스락] 소리 나는) If things such as paper or leaves rustle, or if you rustle them, they move about and make a soft, dry sound.
flutter^{복습} [flʌ́tə:r]	v. (새 등이) 날갯짓하다, (깃발 등이) 펄럭이다; n. 펄럭임 If something light such as a small bird or a piece of paper flutters somewhere, it moves through the air with small quick movements.
beat^{복습} [bi:t]	v. (beat–beaten/beat) (날개를) 퍼덕거리다; 치다, 두드리다; (심장이) 고동치다; n. 퍼덕임; [음악] 박자, 고동 When a bird or insect beats its wings or when its wings beat, its wings move up and down.

cupboard^{복습}
[kʌbərd]

n. 붙박이장, 벽장; 식기장, 찬장
A cupboard is a piece of furniture that has one or two doors, usually contains shelves, and is used to store things.

wardrobe^{복습}
[wɔ́:rdròub]

n. 옷장; 의상
A wardrobe is a tall cupboard or cabinet in which you can hang your clothes.

raggedy
[rǽgidi]

a. 누더기의, 다 찢어진
People and things that are raggedy are dirty and untidy. Raggedy clothes are old and torn.

witch[*]
[wiʧ]

n. 마녀
In fairy stories, a witch is a woman, usually an old woman, who has evil magic powers.

costume[*]
[kástju:m]

n. 의상, 옷차림
An actor's costume is the set of clothes they wear while they are performing.

patch^{복습}
[pætʃ]

v. 헝겊을 대고 깁다; n. 부분, 단편, 파편; 헝겊 조각; 반창고
If you patch something that has a hole in it, you mend it by fastening a patch over the hole.

scarecrow
[skéərkròu]

n. 허수아비
A scarecrow is an object in the shape of a person, which is put in a field where crops are growing in order to frighten birds away.

warrior[*]
[wɔ́:riər]

n. 전사, 무인
A worrior is a soldier who has both experience and skill in fighting, especially in the past.

glitter^{복습}
[glítər]

vi. 반짝반짝 빛나다, 반짝이다; n. 반짝거림, 광채
If something glitters, light comes from or is reflected off different parts of it.

slinky
[slíŋki]

a. (여자의 옷이) 신체의 선을 살린, 날씬하게 드리워진
Slinky clothes fit very closely to a woman's body in a way that makes her look sexually attractive.

drawer^{**}
[drɔ:r]

n. 서랍
A drawer is part of a desk, chest, or other piece of furniture that is shaped like a box and is designed for putting things in.

faint^{복습}
[feint]

a. 희미한, 어렴풋한; vi. 기절하다
A faint sound, color, mark, feeling, or quality has very little strength or intensity.

fabric[*]
[fǽbrik]

n. 직물, 천
Fabric is cloth or other material produced by weaving together cotton, nylon, wool, silk, or other threads.

twinkle[*]
[twíŋkl]

v. 반짝반짝 빛나다; 깜빡이다; n. 반짝거림
If a star or a light twinkles, it shines with an unsteady light which rapidly and constantly changes from bright to faint.

desert**
[dizə:rt]

① v. 버리다, 유기하다; 인적이 끊기다 ② n. 사막, 황무지
(deserted a. 황량한, 사람이 살지 않는)
If people or animals desert a place, they leave it and it becomes empty.

occupy*
[ákjupai]

vt. 차지하다, 점령하다; 종사하다
If a room or something such as a seat is occupied, someone is using it, so that it is not available for anyone else.

pretend***
[priténd]

v. ~인 체하다, 가장하다; a. 가짜의, 꾸민
If you pretend that something is the case, you act in a way that is intended to make people believe that it is the case, although in fact it is not.

vermin
[vá:rmin]

n. 해충, 기생충
Vermin are small animals such as rats and mice which cause problems to humans by carrying disease and damaging crops or food.

vague복습
[veig]

a. 어렴풋한, 막연한
If something written or spoken is vague, it does not explain or express things clearly.

dough
[dou]

n. 반죽 덩어리; 굽지 않는 빵, 가루 반죽
Dough is a fairly firm mixture of flour, water, and sometimes also fat and sugar.

smooth복습
[smu:ð]

v. 반반하게 하다, 매끄럽게 하다; a. 매끄러운; 유창한
If you smooth something, you move your hands over its surface to make it smooth and flat.

bump복습
[bʌmp]

n. 혹; 충돌; v. (쾅 하고) 부딪치다, 충돌하다
A bump on a road is a raised, uneven part.

crack복습
[kræk]

n. 갈라진 금; 갑작스런 날카로운 소리; 조금, 약간; v. 금이 가다, 깨다, 부수다
A crack is a line that appears on the surface of something when it is slightly damaged.

depression*
[dipréʃən]

n. 움푹 파인 곳; 내려 누름; 우울(증), 쇠약; 불황
A depression in a surface is an area which is lower than the parts surrounding it.

demonstrate*
[démənstreit]

vt. 실지로 해보이다; 논증하다, 설명하다
If you demonstrate a particular skill, quality, or feeling, you show by your actions that you have it.

tender*
[téndər]

a. 상냥한, 다정한, 부드러운
Someone or something that is tender expresses gentle and caring feelings.

hospitality**
[hàspətǽləti]

n. 환대, 친절
Hospitality is friendly, welcoming behavior toward guests or people you have just met.

lap*
[læp]

n. 무릎; 한 바퀴; v. 겹치게 하다
If you have something on your lap, it is on top of your legs and near to your body.

embarrass ^{복습}
[embǽrəs]

v. 당황스럽게 만들다, 곤란하게 하다 (embarrassed a. 난처한, 당황한)
If something or someone embarrasses you, they make you feel shy or ashamed.

rattle *
[rǽtl]

v. 왈각달각 소리나다, 덜걱덜걱 움직이다; n. 덜거덕거리는 소리
When something rattles or when you rattle it, it makes short sharp knocking sounds because it is being shaken or it keeps hitting against something hard.

bunch ^{복습}
[bʌntʃ]

n. (과일 등의) 송이, 다발; 다량; 떼, 한패
A bunch of things is a number of things, especially a large number.

plum *
[plʌm]

n. 자두
A plum is a small, sweet fruit with a smooth red or yellow skin and a stone in the middle.

suck **
[sʌk]

v. 빨다, 흡수하다; n. 빨아들임
If something sucks a liquid, gas, or object in a particular direction, it draws the object there with a powerful force.

mantelpiece ^{복습}
[mǽntlpìːs]

n. 벽난로 위 선반
A mantelpiece is a wood or stone shelf which is the top part of a border round a fireplace.

tumble *
[tʌmbl]

v. 굴러 떨어지다, 넘어지다[뜨리다]; n. 추락; 폭락
If someone or something tumbles somewhere, they fall there with a rolling or bouncing movement.

carry on ^{복습}

phrasal v. (임무·일을) 계속하다, (중단된 일 등을) 재개하다
If you carry on doing something, you continue or persevere in doing it.

set off ^{복습}

phrasal v. 출발하다, 시작하다, 착수하다; (알람 등이) 울리다
When you set off for somewhere, you begin a journey to there.

meadow ^{복습}
[médou]

n. 목초지, 초원
A meadow is a field which has grass and flowers growing in it.

crude *
[kruːd]

a. 천연 그대로의, 가공하지 않은; 거친, 투박한
Crude substances are in a natural or unrefined state, and have not yet been used in manufacturing processes.

approximate *
[əprάksəmət]

a. 근접한, 대략의; v. 가까워지다
An approximate number, time, or position is close to the correct number, time, or position, but is not exact.

splodge
[splɑdʒ]

n. 얼룩, 반점 (무늬); v. 얼룩지게 하다
A splodge is a large uneven mark or stain, especially one that has been caused by a liquid.

wonder ^{복습}
[wʌ́ndər]

v. 호기심을 가지다, 이상하게 여기다; n. 경탄할 만한 것, 경이
If you wonder about something, you think about it, either because it interests you and you want to know more about it, or because you are worried or suspicious about it.

proper ^{복습}
[prɑ́pər]

a. 적당[타당]한; 예의 바른; 고유의 (properly ad. 적당히, 알맞게)
The proper thing is the one that is correct or most suitable.

mist^{복습}
[mist]

n. 안개; v. 안개가 끼다, 눈이 흐려지다
Mist consists of a large number of tiny drops of water in the air, which make it difficult to see very far.

explorer^{복습}
[iksplɔ́:rər]

n. 탐험가; 조사자, 검사자
An explorer is someone who travels to places about which very little is known, in order to discover what is there.

pale^{복습}
[péil]

a. 희미한; 창백한; 엷은, 연한; v. 엷어지(게 하)다
If something is pale, it is very light in color or almost white.

enormous^{복습}
[inɔ́:rməs]

a. 엄청난, 거대한, 막대한
You can use enormous to emphasize the great degree or extent of something.

texture*
[tékstʃər]

n. 감촉, 질감; 직물; 직조법, 짜임새; 조직, 구성, 구조
The texture of something is the way that it feels when you touch it, for example how smooth or rough it is.

blind^{복습}
[bláind]

a. 눈먼, 장님인; 맹목적인; v. (잠시) 앞이 안보이게 만들다; 눈이 멀게하다
Someone who is blind is unable to see because their eyes are damaged.

plain**
[plein]

a. 분명한, 명백한; 무늬가 없는, 꾸밈없는; n. 평지, 평야
(plain as day idiom 낮의 빛과 같이 명료한, 분명한)
If a fact, situation, or statement is plain, it is easy to recognize or understand.

pad^{복습}
[pæd]

① v. 거닐다, 발소리를 내지 않고 걷다; ② vt. ~에 덧대다; n. 덧대는 것, 패드
When someone pads somewhere, they walk there with steps that are fairly quick, light, and quiet.

tower*
[táuər]

vi. 높이 솟다; (~보다) 뛰어나다; n. 탑
Someone or something that towers over surrounding people or things is a lot taller than they are.

loom*
[lu:m]

vi. 어렴풋이 나타나다, 흐릿하게 보이다; (위험·근심 등이) 불안하게 다가오다
If something looms over you, it appears as a large or unclear shape, often in a frightening way.

precise^{복습}
[prisáis]

a. 정확한, 정밀한; 명확한 (precisely ad. 정확히, 정밀하게)
You use precise to emphasize that you are referring to an exact thing, rather than something vague.

curl**
[kə:rl]

vt. 꼬다, 곱슬곱슬하게 하다; n. 컬, 곱슬머리
If your toes, fingers, or other parts of your body curl, or if you curl them, they form a curved or round shape.

indeed^{복습}
[indíd]

ad. 실로, 참으로, 과연, 정말
You use indeed to confirm or agree with something that has just been said.

shiver*
[ʃívər]

v. (추위·공포로) 후들후들 떨다; 전율하다; n. 떨림, 전율
When you shiver, your body shakes slightly because you are cold or frightened.

70

impress^{복습}
[imprés]

v. ~에게 (깊은) 인상을 주다; 감동시키다
(unimpressed a. 대단하다고 생각하지 않는; 감명받지 않은)
If something impresses you, you feel great admiration for it.

clump^{복습}
[klʌmp]

n. 수풀, (관목의) 덤불
A clump of things such as trees or plants is a small group of them growing together.

hang on^{복습}

idiom 잠깐 기다리세요; phrasal v. 꽉 붙잡다, 단단히 매달리다
If you ask someone to hang on, you ask them to wait or stop what they are doing or saying for a moment.

leap^{복습}
[liːp]

n. 뜀, 도약; v. 껑충 뛰다, 뛰어넘다
If you leap, you jump high in the air or jump a long distance.

at the best of times

idiom (보통 부정문에서) 가장 좋은 때[상황, 상태]에도
You say at the best of times when you are making a negative or critical comment to emphasize that it is true even when the circumstances are as favorable as possible.

spy[*]
[spai]

n. 스파이; v. 염탐하다, 몰래 조사하다
A spy is a person whose job is to find out secret information about another country or organization.

bound[*]
[baund]

① n. 뜀, 도약, 반동; v. 뛰어가다; 튀어 오르다 ② n. 경계, 범위
A bound is a long or high jump.

bat^{복습}
[bæt]

① v. (배트 · 막대기로) 치다; n. (야구의) 배트, 막대기; ② n. 박쥐
When you bat, you have a turn at hitting the ball with a bat in baseball, softball, cricket, or rounders.

claw[*]
[klɔː]

n. (날카롭고 굽은) 갈고리발톱, 집게발 v. 발톱으로 할퀴다
(clawed a. 손톱[발톱]이 있는)
The claws of a bird or animal are the thin, hard, curved nails at the end of its feet.

torture[*]
[tɔ́ːrtʃər]

vt. 고문하다, 고통을 주다; n. 고문, 고뇌
To torture someone means to cause them to suffer mental pain or anxiety.

stumble[*]
[stʌmbl]

v. 비틀거리며 걷다, 발부리가 걸리다; n. 비틀거림
If you stumble, you put your foot down awkwardly while you are walking or running and nearly fall over.

daze
[deiz]

vt. 멍하게 하다; 현혹시키다; n. 멍한 상태; 눈이 부심 (dazed a. 멍한)
To daze means to make someone feel confused or unable to think clearly.

tendency^{**}
[téndənsi]

n. 경향, 추세
A tendency is a worrying or unpleasant habit or action that keeps occurring.

mercy[*]
[mɔ́ːrsi]

n. 자비, 연민 (merciful a. 자비로운, 관대한)
If someone in authority shows mercy, they choose not to harm someone they have power over, or they forgive someone they have the right to punish.

permit[***]
[pərmít]
v. 허가하다, 허락하다
If someone permit you to do something, they allow you to do it.

occasional[복습]
[əkéiʒənl]
a. 가끔의, 때때로의
Occasional means happening sometimes, but not regularly or often.

mote
[mout]
n. (아주 작은) 티끌
A mote is a tiny piece of a substance.

reflect[복습]
[riflékt]
v. 비추다; 반사하다, 반영하다; 깊이 생각하다, 심사숙고하다
When something is reflected in a mirror or in water, you can see its image in the mirror or in the water.

serpent
[sə́:rpənt]
n. (특히 큰) 뱀
A serpent is a snake.

gratitude[**]
[grǽtətjù:d]
n. 감사, 고마움 (ingratitude n. 은혜를 모름, 배은망덕)
Gratitude is the state of feeling grateful.

waggle
[wǽgl]
v. 흔들다, 좌우로 움직이다
If you waggle something, or if something waggles, it moves up and down or from side to side with short quick movements.

caress
[kərés]
v. 어루만지다, 쓰다듬다
If you caress someone, you stroke them gently and affectionately.

no matter what
idiom 무슨 일이 있어도, 비록 무엇이 ∼할지라도
You use 'no matter what' to say that something is true or happens in all circumstances.

lounge[*]
[laundʒ]
n. 휴게실, 로비, 라운지; v. 빈둥거리며 시간을 보내다; 편하게 앉다
In a house, a lounge is a room where people sit and relax.

extend[**]
[iksténd]
v. (손·발 등을) 뻗다, 늘이다; 넓어지다, 퍼지다
If an object extends from a surface or place, it sticks out from it.

crawl[복습]
[krɔ:l]
vi. 기어가다, 느릿느릿 가다; n. 기어감; 서행
When you crawl, you move forward on your hands and knees.

suit yourself[복습]
idiom 마음대로 해라, 네 멋대로 해라
If you say 'suit yourself', you tell somebody to do what they want, even though it annoys you.

particular[복습]
[pərtíkjələr]
a. 특정한, 특별한, 특유의 (particularly ad. 특히, 두드러지게)
You use particular to emphasize that you are talking about one thing or one kind of thing rather than other similar ones.

neat[**]
[ni:t]
a. 산뜻한, 깔끔한 (neatly ad. 깔끔하게)
A neat place, thing, or person is tidy and smart, and has everything in the correct place.

ashtray[복습]
[ǽʃtrèi]
n. (담배) 재떨이
An ashtray is a container into which people who smoke put ash, cigarette ends, etc.

pop[복습]
[pap]
v. (물건을) 쏙 넣다; 뻥 하고 터지다; 불쑥 움직이다; n. 뻥[탁] 하는 소리; 발포
If you pop something somewhere, you put it there quickly.

72

crunch
[krʌntʃ]

v. 우두둑 깨물다 (부수다), (무엇을 으스러뜨리는 소리를 내며) 가다;
n. 우두둑 부서지는 소리
If you crunch something hard, such as a sweet, you crush it noisily between your teeth.

weird*
[wiərd]

a. 이상한, 기묘한; 수상한
If you describe something or someone as weird, you mean that they are strange.

ignore^{복습}
[ignɔ́:r]

vt. 무시하다, 모르는 체하다
If you ignore someone or something, you pay no attention to them.

overexcite
[òuvəriksáit]

vt. 과도하게 흥분시키다, 너무 자극시키다 (overexcited a. 지나치게 흥분한)
Overexcited means too excited and not behaving in a calm or sensible way.

embroidery
[imbrɔ́idəri]

n. 자수, 수(놓기); (이야기 따위의) 윤색, 과장
Embroidery is the activity of stitching designs onto cloth.

tuck*
[tʌk]

v. 밀어 넣다, 쑤셔 넣다; n. 접어 넣은 단
If you tuck something somewhere, you put it there so that it is safe, comfortable, or neat.

purse^{복습}
[pə:rs]

v. (입을) 오므리다; (눈살을) 찌푸리다; n. 지갑
If you purse your lips, you move them into a small, rounded shape, usually because you disapprove of something or when you are thinking.

raisin*
[réizn]

n. 건포도
Raisins are dried grapes.

hazel
[héizəl]

a. 엷은 갈색의
Hazel eyes are greenish-brown in color.

twine
[twain]

v. (~을) 휘감(기게 하)다; n. 꼰 실; 꼬기, 감김; 엉클어짐, 뒤얽힘
If you twine one thing around another, or if one thing twines around another, the first thing is twisted or wound around the second.

frown*
[fraun]

vi. 얼굴을 찡그리다, 눈살을 찌푸리다; n. 찌푸린 얼굴
When someone frowns, their eyebrows become drawn together, because they are annoyed or puzzled.

toss*
[tɔ:s]

v. 던지다, 내던지다
If you toss something somewhere, you throw it there lightly, often in a rather careless way.

triumphant^{복습}
[traiʌmfənt]

a. 의기양양한; 크게 성공한, 큰 승리를 거둔 (triumphantly ad. 의기양양하여)
Someone who is triumphant has gained a victory or succeeded in something and feels very happy about it.

advance**
[ædvǽns]

v. 전진하다, 나아가다; 진보하다
To advance means to move forward, often in order to attack someone.

reveal^{복습}
[riví:l]

vt. 드러내다, 보이다, 나타내다
If you reveal something that has been out of sight, you uncover it so that people can see it.

dim^{복습}
[dim]

a. 어둑한, 흐릿한, 희미한; **v.** 어둑하게 하다, 흐려지다
A dim place is rather dark because there is not much light in it.

fragment[*]
[frǽgmənt]

n. 부서진 조각, 파편, 떨어져 나간 조각
A fragment of something is a small piece or part of it.

stick^{복습}
[stik]

① **v.** 달라붙다, 붙이다; 찔러 넣다, 찌르다; 꽂히다, 박히다 ② **n.** 막대기, 지팡이
If one thing sticks to another, it becomes attached to it and is difficult to remove.

74

chapter seven

1. Which of the following does NOT describe the space Coraline entered?
   A. It was about the size of a broom closet.
   B. One of the walls was glass.
   C. There was a switch on the wall.
   D. There was a spider.

2. The children in the room had lost many things. Which of the following is something that they had NOT lost?
   A. Their hearts
   B. Their breath
   C. Their names
   D. Their memories

3. Why were the other children in the room?
   A. The other mother wanted them all to be friends.
   B. The other mother put them there and forgot about them.
   C. They were playing and got trapped in there.
   D. They are happy to be in there and stayed for a long time.

4. Why are the children unable to leave?

   A. They forgot where they needed to go.

   B. The other mother had eaten their souls.

   C. They can leave but don't really want to go.

   D. The other mother had taken and hidden their souls somewhere.

5. Why did Coraline believe that she wouldn't be kept in the darkness forever?

   A. The other mother brought her there to play games and wanted a challenge.

   B. The other mother would make dinner for her when she got hungry.

   C. She would find a way out on her own.

   D. The other father would let her out.

6. What advice did Coraline receive from a ghostly whisper?

   A. Challenge the other mother.

   B. Flee while you still can.

   C. Look through the stone.

   D. Find the souls of the children.

$$\frac{1{,}294 \text{ words}}{\text{reading time (\quad) sec}} \times 60 = (\quad) \text{ WPM}$$

Build Your Vocabulary

sob*
[sɑb]

n. 흐느낌, 오열; v. 흐느껴 울다
A sob is one of the noises that you make when you are crying.

well^{복습}
[wel]

v. 솟아 나오다, 내뿜다, 분출하다; n. 우물
If liquids, for example tears, well, they come to the surface and form a pool.

imprison*
[imprízn]

vt. 가두다, 구속하다, 수감하다
If someone is imprisoned, they are locked up or kept somewhere, usually in prison as a punishment for a crime or for political opposition.

broom^{복습}
[bru:m]

n. 비, 빗자루
A broom is a kind of brush with a long handle.

lie^{복습}
[lai]

vi. 눕다, 누워 있다; 놓여 있다, 위치하다
If you are lying somewhere, you are in a horizontal position and are not standing or sitting.

surface^{복습}
[sə́:rfis]

n. 표면, 외관; a. 표면의
The surface of something is the flat top part of it or the outside of it.

doorknob^{복습}
[dɔ́:rnàb]

n. 문손잡이
A doorknob is a round handle on a door.

conceal*
[kənsí:l]

vt. 감추다, 비밀로 하다
If you conceal something, you cover it or hide it carefully.

scuttle^{복습}
[skʌtl]

vi. 급히 가다, 황급히 달리다; 허둥지둥 도망가다
When people or small animals scuttle somewhere, they run there with short quick steps.

choke**
[tʃouk]

v. 숨이 막히다, 질식시키다; n. 질식
When you choke or when something chokes you, you cannot breathe properly or get enough air into your lungs.

shriek*
[ʃríːk]

n. 비명; v. 새된 소리를 지르다, 비명을 지르다
A shriek is a high-pitched piercing sound or words as an expression of terror, pain, or excitement.

pitch dark
[pítʃ dɑ́:rk]

a. 칠흑같이 새까만[어두운]
If a place or the night is pitch dark, it is completely dark.

78

whisper^{복습}
[hwíspə:r]

v. 속삭이다
When you whisper, you say something very quietly.

hush^{복습}
[hʌʃ]

int. 쉿. 조용히 해; v. 침묵하다; 잠잠하게 하다; n. 침묵, 고요함
You say 'Hush!' to someone when you are asking or telling them to be quiet.

shush
[ʃʌʃ]

int. 쉿. 조용히; v. 쉬잇 하여 입 다물게 하다;
You say shush when you are telling someone to be quiet.

beat^{복습}
[bi:t]

n. 퍼덕임; [음악] 박자, 고동;
v. (날개를) 퍼덕거리다; 치다, 두드리다; (심장이) 고동치다
When a bird or insect beats its wings or when its wings beat, its wings move up and down.

moth[*]
[mɔ:θ]

n. [곤충] 나방
A moth is an insect like a butterfly which usually flies about at night.

hesitant
[hézətənt]

a. 주저하는; 머뭇거리는, 망설이는
If you are hesitant about doing something, you do not do it quickly or immediately.

faraway[*]
[fɑ́:rəwèi]

a. 먼, 멀리 떨어진
A faraway place is a long distance from you or from a particular place.

governess
[gʌ́vərnis]

n. (아이들의 예절·교육을 맡는) 여자 가정교사
A governess is a woman who is employed by a family to live with them and educate their children.

hoop
[hu:p]

n. 테, 링, 굴렁쇠
A large ring made of wood, metal, or plastic.

bob
[bɑb]

v. 위아래로 움직이다, 까딱까딱 흔들리다
If something bobs, it moves up and down, like something does when it is floating on water.

breeze[*]
[bri:z]

n. 산들바람, 미풍; vi. 산들산들 불다
A breeze is a gentle wind.

ember
[émbər]

n. (pl.) (꺼져가는 불 속의) 붉은 석탄[장작], 타다 남은 것
The embers of a fire are small pieces of wood or coal that remain and glow with heat after the fire has finished burning.

nursery[*]
[nə́:rsəri]

n. 육아실, 탁아소, 보육원; 양성소, 훈련소
A nursery is a place where children who are not old enough to go to school are looked after.

squeeze^{복습}
[skwi:z]

vt. 꽉 쥐다, 짜다, 압착하다; 쑤셔 넣다; n. 압착, 짜냄
If you squeeze something, you press it firmly, usually with your hands.

pause^{복습}
[pɔ:z]

n. 멈춤, 중지; vi. 중단하다, 잠시 멈추다
A pause is a short period when you stop doing something before continuing.

curl^{복습}
[kə:rl]

vt. 곱슬곱슬하게 하다, 꼬다; n. 컬, 곱슬머리
If your hair curls or if you curl it, it is full of tight curves and spirals.

doubt^{복습}
[daut]

n. 의심; 회의; v. 의심하다, 의혹을 품다 (doubtfully ad. 미심쩍게, 의심스럽게)
If you have doubt or doubts about something, you feel uncertain about it and do not know whether it is true or possible.

glow^{복습}
[glou]

v. 빛을 내다; n. 빛, 밝음
If something glows, it produces a dull, steady light.

reckon[*]
[rékən]

vt. 세다, 계산하다; ~라고 생각하다
If something is reckoned to be a particular figure, it is calculated to be roughly that amount.

parlor^{복습}
[páːrlər]

n. 거실, 응접실; 영업실
A parlor is a room in a house where people can sit and talk and relax.

flee[*]
[fliː]

vi. 달아나다, 도망치다; 사라지다
If you flee from something or someone, or flee a person or thing, you escape from them.

fancy^{**}
[fǽnsi]

v. 공상[상상]하다; 좋아하다; n. 공상; 기호, 선호; a. 화려한, 고급스러운
To fancy means to feel a desire or liking for, to imagine.

vein[*]
[vein]

n. 혈관, 정맥; 기질, 특질
Your veins are the thin tubes in your body through which your blood flows toward your heart.

husk
[hʌsk]

n. (곡물의) 겉껍질; v. ~의 껍질을 벗기다
A husk is the outer covering of a grain or a seed.

mistress[*]
[místris]

n. 여자 주인, 권한을 가진 여자
A dog's mistress is the woman or girl who owns it.

figure^{***}
[fígjər]

n. 모습, 인물; 숫자, 계산; 도형, 도표; v. 계산하다; 생각하다, 판단하다
You refer to someone that you can see as a figure when you cannot see them clearly or when you are describing them.

pulse[*]
[pʌls]

v. 고동치다, 맥이 뛰다; n. 맥박, 고동; 파동
If something pulses, it moves, appears, or makes a sound with a strong regular rhythm.

afterimage
[ǽftərimidʒ]

n. 잔상(殘像)
Afterimage is an image that persists for a time after one has stopped looking at an object.

wisp^{복습}
[wisp]

n. 작은 단[묶음]; 한 조각
A wisp of something such as smoke or cloud is an amount of it in a long thin shape.

hollow^{**}
[hálou]

a. (소리 따위가) 공허한, 속이 빈; 오목한; n. 구멍; 움푹한 곳; v. 속이 비다
If you describe a statement, situation, or person as hollow, you mean they have no real value, worth, or effectiveness.

challenge^{복습}
[tʃǽlindʒ]

n. 도전; v. 도전하다
A challenge is something new and difficult which requires great effort and determination.

bend**
[bend]

v. 구부리다, 굽히다, 숙이다; n. 커브, 굽음, 굽은 곳
When you bend, you move the top part of your body downward and forward.

cramp
[kræmp]

vt. 속박하다, 제한하다, 가두다; n. 꺾쇠, 죔쇠 (cramped a. 비좁은, 갑갑한)
To cramp means to restrict or prevent them from acting freely or creatively.

strike***
[straik]

v. (struck–struck) ~이 생각나다; 치다, 찌르다; 습격하다; n. 공격, 공습; 파업
If an idea or thought strikes you, it suddenly comes into your mind.

barely^{복습}
[béərli]

ad. 간신히, 가까스로; 거의 ~ 않다
You use barely to say that something is only just true or only just the case.

shrivel^{복습}
[ʃríːvəl]

v. 쪼글쪼글해지다, 주름(살)지다, 줄어들다
When something shrivels or when something shrivels it, it becomes dryer and smaller, often with lines in its surface, as a result of losing the water it contains.

tender^{복습}
[téndər]

a. 부드러운, 상냥한, 다정한 (tenderly ad. 상냥하게)
Someone or something that is tender expresses gentle and caring feelings.

chapter eight

1. Why didn't Coraline resist the mother carrying her from the dark room into the kitchen?
   A. She was hungry and wanted to see what the other mother cooked for her.
   B. She had finally given up against the other mother.
   C. She was only conscious of being cuddled and loved.
   D. She tried to treat the other mother as her real mother.

2. How did the other mother react when Coraline mentioned the other children she met in the cupboard?
   A. She remembered them well and told Coraline that she will be treated differently.
   B. She acted as if she didn't know about them.
   C. She told Coraline that ghosts aren't real.
   D. She said she would let them out of the darkness now.

3. Which of the following was NOT one of the promises Coraline made if she lost the game?
   A. She would stay with the other mother forever.
   B. She would play Happy Families.
   C. She would let the other mother sew buttons into her eyes.
   D. She would forget about her real parents.

4. What kind of game did Coraline suggest playing with the other mother?
   A. A riddle game
   B. A test of knowledge
   C. An exploring game
   D. A fighting game

5. Why did Coraline make the other mother swear on something besides her mother's grave?
   A. The other mother buried her mother alive.
   B. The other mother ran away from her mother.
   C. The other mother didn't have a real mother.
   D. The other mother didn't make promises.

6. How did Coraline find the first soul?
   A. She used the snow globe to bring the first soul to her from the drawing room.
   B. She asked the cat where she should begin to look, and it suggested the toy box .
   C. She asked the children she met where to look, and they suggested the toy box.
   D. She looked through the stone and saw that the marble from the toy box was glowing.

7. How did Coraline know the creature in the theater couldn't harm her?
   A. It was the real Miss Spink and Miss Forcible.
   B. It was attached to the wall and couldn't chase her.
   C. It told Coraline that it wouldn't hurt her.
   D. It was really tired and wouldn't attack Coraline.

1분에 몇 단어를 읽는지 리딩 속도를 측정해보세요.

$$\frac{3,331 \ words}{reading \ time \ (\quad) \ sec} \times 60 = (\qquad) \ WPM$$

Build Your Vocabulary

blush*
[blʌʃ]

n. 얼굴을 붉힘, 홍조; v. 얼굴을 붉히다, (얼굴이) 빨개지다
When you blush, your face becomes redder than usual because you are ashamed or embarrassed.

wriggle
[rigl]

v. 꿈틀거리다, 몸부림치다; n. 몸부림침, 꿈틀거림
If you wriggle or wriggle part of your body, you twist and turn with quick movements.

polish^{복습}
[páliʃ]

v. 닦다, 윤내다; n. 광택, 세련; 광택제
If you polish something, you rub it with a cloth to make it shine.

solid**
[sálid]

a. 단단한; 견실한, 견고한; n. 고체
A substance that is solid is very hard or firm.

cradle*
[kreidl]

v. (안전하게 보호하듯이) 떠받치다, 살짝 안다; n. 요람, 유아용 침대
If you cradle someone or something in your arms or hands, you hold them carefully and gently.

countertop
[káuntərtàp]

n. (부엌의) 조리대
A countertop is a flat surface in a kitchen which is easily cleaned and on which you can prepare food.

struggle**
[strʌgl]

v. 분투하다, 발버둥 치다, 몸부림치다; n. 투쟁, 분투
If you struggle to do something, you try hard to do it, even though other people or things may be making it difficult for you to succeed.

conscious**
[kánʃəs]

a. 의식하고 있는, 알고 있는, 지각 있는
If you are conscious of something, you notice it or realize that it is happening.

cuddle
[kʌdl]

v. 꼭 껴안다, 껴안고 귀여워하다
If you cuddle someone, you put your arms round them and hold them close as a way of showing your affection.

fetch**
[fetʃ]

vt. 데려오다, 불러오다, 가져오다
If you fetch something or someone, you go and get them from the place where they are.

cupboard^{복습}
[kʌbərd]

n. 붙박이장, 벽장, 식기장, 찬장
A cupboard is a piece of furniture that has one or two doors, usually contains shelves, and is used to store things.

temper**
[témpər]

v. 누그러뜨리다, 완화하다; n. 기질, 성질, 화, 노여움
To temper means to soften something or make it less severe.

84

justice**
[dʒʌ́stis]

n. 정의, 공정
Justice is fairness in the way that people are treated.

mercy^{복습}
[mə́:rsi]

n. 자비, 연민
If someone in authority shows mercy, they choose not to harm someone they have power over, or they forgive someone they have the right to punish.

sinner
[sínər]

n. 죄인, 죄 있는 사람
A sinner is a person who has committed a sin or sins.

compliant
[kəmpláiənt]

a. 유순한, 시키는 대로 하는, 고분고분한
If you say that someone is compliant, you mean they willingly do what they are asked to do.

fair-spoken
[féər-spóukən]

a. (말씨가) 정중한, 상냥한
If you are fair-spoken, you are bland and civil in language and address.

scratch^{복습}
[skrætʃ]

v. 긁다, 할퀴다; n. 생채기, 할큄, 찰과상
If you scratch yourself, you rub your fingernails against your skin because it is itching.

grit
[grit]

n. 티끌, 먼지, 모래; v. 이를 갈다; 쓸리다, 삐걱삐걱 (소리 나게) 하다
Grit is very small particles of a hard material, especially of stone or sand.

bustle
[bʌ́sl]

v. 부산하게 움직이다, 법석떨다; 재촉하다; n. 야단법석, 소란
If someone bustles somewhere, they move there in a hurried way, often because they are very busy.

slab
[slæb]

n. (빵·고기 등의) 넓적하고 두꺼운 조각; 석판, 널빤지
A slab of something is a large, thick, flat piece of it.

shell^{복습}
[ʃel]

n. 껍데기; 조가비; v. 껍데기를 벗기다
The shell of a nut or egg is the hard covering which surrounds it.

crack^{복습}
[kræk]

v. 깨다, 부수다; 금이 가다; n. 조금, 약간; 갈라진 금; 갑작스런 날카로운 소리
When you crack something that has a shell, such as an egg or a nut, you break the shell in order to reach the inside part.

whisk
[hwisk]

v. (달걀 등을) 휘젓다, 휘저어 거품을 내다; (먼지 등을) 털다, 털어내다; n. 털기
If you whisk something such as eggs or cream, you stir it very fast, often with an electric device, so that it becomes full of small bubbles.

whirl*
[hwə́:rl]

v. 빙글 돌다[돌리다], 선회하다
If something or someone whirls around or if you whirl them around, they move around or turn around very quickly.

pat*
[pæt]

n. (납작하고 네모진) 작은 덩어리; 쓰다듬기; v. 톡톡 가볍게 치다, 쓰다듬다
A pat of butter or something else that is soft is a small lump of it.

hiss^{복습}
[his]

v. 쉿 하는 소리를 내다; n. 쉿 (제지·힐책의 소리)
To hiss means to make a sound like a long 's'.

fizzle
[fízl]

v. (특히 불에 타고 있는 것이) 쉬익쉬익 하는 소리를 내다
To fizzle means to make a feeble hissing or spluttering sound.

spin**
[spin]

v. (spun–spun) 돌(리)다, 맴돌(리)다; 오래[질질] 끌다; n. 회전
If something spins or if you spin it, it turns quickly around a central point.

sensible^{복습}
[sénsəbl]

a. 상식적인, 분별 있는; 느낄 수 있는
Sensible people behave in a reasonable way than an emotional one.

liar*
[làiər]

n. 거짓말쟁이
If you say that someone is a liar, you mean that they tell lies.

sizzle
[sizl]

v. (튀김이나 고기 구울 때) 지글지글하다
If something such as hot oil or fat sizzles, it makes hissing sounds.

spit*
[spit]

v. 탁탁[지글지글] 소리내다; 내뱉듯이 말하다; (침 등을) 뱉다; n. 침
To spit means to make a sizzling sound.

fair and square

idiom 공명정대하게, 정정당당하게
If you say that someone won a competition fair and square, you mean that they won honestly and without cheating.

unconcerned
[ʌnkənsɔ́:rnd]

a. 개의치 않는, 무심한, 흥미 없는 (unconcernedness n. 무관심, 무심함)
If a person is unconcerned about something, usually something that most people would care about, they are not interested in it or worried about it.

twitch
[twitʃ]

vi. (손가락 · 근육 따위가) 씰룩거리다; 홱 잡아 당기다, 잡아채다
If a part of your body twitches, or if you twitch it, it makes a sudden quick movement, sometimes one that you cannot control.

drum**
[drʌm]

v. (북을 치듯) 계속 두드리다; 북을 치다; n. 북, 드럼
If something drums on a surface, or if you drum something on a surface, it hits it regularly, making a continuous beating sound.

scarlet*
[skáːrlit]

a. 주홍[진홍]색의; n. 주홍[진홍]색
Something that is scarlet is bright red.

grip
[grip]

v. 꽉 잡다, 움켜잡다; n. 잡음, 움켜쥠; 손잡이
If you grip something, you take hold of it with your hand and continue to hold it firmly.

dutiful
[djúːtifəl]

a. 본분을 지키는, 충실한, 순종하는
If you say that someone is dutiful, you mean that they do everything that they are expected to do.

sew^{복습}
[sou]

v. 바느질하다, 꿰매다, 깁다
When you sew something such as clothes, you make them or repair them by joining pieces of cloth together by passing thread through them with a needle.

trap*
[træp]

v. 좁은 장소에 가두다; 함정에 빠뜨리다; n. 덫, 함정
If you are trapped somewhere, something falls onto you or blocks your way and prevents you from moving or escaping.

slip^{복습}
[slip]

v. 슬며시 두다; 살짝 나오다[들어가다]; 미끄러지다
If you slip something somewhere, you put it there quickly in a way that does not attract attention.

flip ^{복습}
[flip]

v. 홱 뒤집다, 튕겨 올리다, (책 등을) 휙휙 넘기다; n. 손가락으로 튕김
If something flips over, or if you flip it over or into a different position, it moves or is moved into a different position.

frothy
[frɔ́:θi]

a. 거품투성이의, 거품 같은
A frothy liquid has lots of bubbles on its surface.

riddle *
[rídl]

n. 수수께끼
A riddle is a puzzle or joke in which you ask a question that seems to be nonsense but which has a clever or amusing answer.

explore ^{복습}
[iksplɔ́:r]

v. 탐험[답사] 하다, 탐구하다, 조사하다
If you explore a place, you travel around it to find out what it is like.

hesitate ^{복습}
[hézətèit]

v. 주저하다, 머뭇거리다, 망설이다
If you hesitate, you do not speak or act for a short time, usually because you are uncertain, embarrassed, or worried about what you are going to say or do.

triumphant ^{복습}
[traiʌmfənt]

a. 의기양양한; 크게 성공한, 큰 승리를 거둔 (triumphantly ad. 의기양양하여)
Someone who is triumphant has gained a victory or succeeded in something and feels very happy about it.

wonder ^{복습}
[wʌ́ndə:r]

v. 호기심을 가지다, 이상하게 여기다; n. 경탄할 만한 것, 경이
If you wonder about something, you think about it, either because it interests you and you want to know more about it, or because you are worried or suspicious about it.

give in

phrasal v. 굴복하다, 따르다, 항복하다
If you give in, you admit that you are defeated or that you cannot do something.

starve ^{복습}
[staːrv]

v. 굶주리다, 굶어죽다
If people starve, they suffer greatly from lack of food which sometimes leads to their death.

swear **
[swɛər]

v. 맹세하다, 단언하다; 욕을 하다; n. 맹세, 선서
If you swear to do something, you promise in a serious way that you will do it.

crawl ^{복습}
[krɔːl]

vi. 기어가다, 느릿느릿 가다; n. 기어감; 서행
When you crawl, you move forward on your hands and knees.

waggle ^{복습}
[wǽgl]

v. 흔들다, 좌우로 움직이다
If you waggle something, or if something waggles, it moves up and down or from side to side with short quick movements.

display ^{복습}
[displéi]

v. 보이다, 나타내다, 진열(전시)하다; n. 진열품, 전시
If you display something, you show it to people.

claw ^{복습}
[klɔː]

n. (날카롭고 굽은) 갈고리발톱, 집게발; v. 발톱으로 할퀴다 (clawlike a. 갈퀴모양의)
The claws of a bird or animal are the thin, hard, curved nails at the end of its feet.

shrug *
[ʃrʌg]

v. (양 손바닥을 내보이면서 어깨를) 으쓱하다; n. 으쓱하기
If you shrug, you raise your shoulders to show that you are not interested in something or that you do not know or care about something.

wolf*
[wulf]

vt. ~을 게걸스럽게 먹다, 정신없이 먹다
When you wolf something down, you eat it very quickly, especially in large quantities.

expression^{복습}
[ikspréʃən]

n. 표정, 표현, 표현법
Your expression is the way that your face looks at a particular moment. It shows what you are thinking or feeling.

abandon^{복습}
[əbǽndən]

vt. 버리다; 단념하다, 그만두다 (abandoned **a.** 버려진, 황폐한)
If you abandon a place, thing, or person, you leave the place, thing, or person permanently or for a long time.

bottomless
[bátəmlis]

a. 바닥이 안 보이는; 무한한
If you describe something as bottomless, you mean that it is so deep that it seems to have no bottom.

peer^{복습}
[piər]

vi. 응시하다, 자세히 보다
If you peer at something, you look at it very hard.

freezer^{복습}
[frí:zər]

n. 냉동고
A freezer is a large container like a fridge in which the temperature is kept below freezing point so that you can store food inside it for long periods.

poke*
[pouk]

v. 찌르다, 쑤시다; **n.** 찌름, 쑤심
If you poke someone or something, you quickly push them with your finger or with a sharp object.

compartment^{복습}
[kəmpá:rtmənt]

n. 구획, 칸막이
A compartment is one of the separate parts of an object that is used for keeping things in.

smirk
[smə:rk]

n. 능글맞은 웃음; **vi.** 능글맞게 웃다
A smirk is an unpleasant smile.

hover*
[hávər]

v. 공중을 맴돌다; 배회하다; **n.** 공중을 떠다님; 배회
To hover means to stay in the same position in the air without moving forward or backward.

edge^{복습}
[edʒ]

n. 가장자리, 변두리, 끝; **v.** 조금씩[살살] 움직이다[이동시키다]; 테두리를 두르다
The edge of something is the place or line where it stops, or the part of it that is furthest from the middle.

lean^{복습}
[li:n]

① **v.** 기울다, 상체를 굽히다; 의지하다; ~을 기대어 세우다 ② **a.** 야윈, 마른
If you lean on or against someone or something, you rest against them so that they partly support your weight.

crimson
[krímzn]

a. 진홍색의; **n.** 진홍색
Something that is crimson is deep red in color.

varnish
[vá:rniʃ]

v. 매니큐어를 칠하다, 광택을 내다; **n.** 니스, 광택제
If you varnish something, you paint it with an oily liquid which gives it a hard, clear, shiny surface.

tap^{복습}
[tæp]

① **v.** 가볍게 두드리다; **n.** 가볍게 두드리기 ② **n.** 주둥이, (수도 등의) 꼭지
If you tap something, you hit it with a quick light blow or a series of quick light blows.

surface^{복습}
[sə́:rfis]

n. 표면, 외관; **a.** 표면의
The surface of something is the flat top part of it or the outside of it.

ripe*
[raip]

a. 익은, 여문
Ripe fruit or grain is fully grown and ready to eat.

relentless
[riléntlis]

a. 끊임없는, 집요한; 냉혹한, 잔인한, 가차없는
Something bad that is relentless never stops or never becomes less intense.

droplet
[dráplit]

n. 작은 물방울
A droplet is a very small drop of liquid.

faucet*
[fɔ́:sit]

n. (수도·통의) 물 꼭지, 물 주둥이
A faucet is a device that controls the flow of a liquid or gas from a pipe or container.

sink^{복습}
[siŋk]

n. (부엌의) 싱크대, 개수대; **v.** 가라앉다, 빠지다; 밀어넣다, 가라앉히다
A sink is a large fixed container in a kitchen, with taps to supply water. It is mainly used for washing dishes.

shiver^{복습}
[ʃívə:r]

v. (추위·공포로) 후들후들 떨다; 전율하다; **n.** 떨림, 전율
When you shiver, your body shakes slightly because you are cold or frightened.

prefer^{복습}
[prifə́r]

vt. ~을 좋아하다, 차라리 ~을 택하다
If you prefer someone or something, you like that person or thing better than another, and so you are more likely to choose them if there is a choice.

location*
[loukéiʃən]

n. 위치, 소재, 거주지
The location of someone or something is their exact position.

reassure^{복습}
[ri:əʃúər]

vt. 안심시키다 (reassuring **a.** 안심시키는, 위안을 주는)
If you reassure someone, you say or do things to make them stop worrying about something.

glance^{복습}
[glæns]

v. 흘긋 보다, 잠깐 보다; **n.** 흘긋 봄
If you glance at something or someone, you look at them very quickly and then look away again immediately.

indistinct
[indistíŋkt]

a. (형상·기억 등이) 뚜렷하지 않은, 희미한
Something that is indistinct is unclear and difficult to see, hear, or recognize.

coal*
[koul]

n. 석탄
Coal is a hard black substance that is extracted from the ground and burned as fuel.

nondescript
[nàndiskrípt]

a. 정체를 알 수 없는, 별 특징 없는
If you describe something or someone as nondescript, you mean that their appearance is rather dull, and not at all interesting or attractive.

pebble^{복습}
[pebl]

n. 조약돌, 자갈
A pebble is a small, smooth, round stone which is found on beaches and at the bottom of rivers.

glimmer
[glímər]

vi. 희미하게 빛나다, 깜빡이다; n. 희미한 빛
If something glimmers, it produces or reflects a faint, gentle, often unsteady light.

trail*
[treil]

n. 지나간 자국, 흔적; v. 끌(리)다; ~을 뒤쫓다
A trail is a series of marks or other signs of movement or other activities left by someone or something.

drift^{복습}
[drift]

v. 표류하다, 떠돌다; n. 표류; 경향, 추세
When something drifts somewhere, it is carried there by the movement of wind or water.

flutter^{복습}
[flʌtəːr]

v. (깃발 등이) 펄럭이다, (새 등이) 날갯짓하다; n. 펄럭임
If something thin or light flutters, or if you flutter it, it moves up and down or from side to side with a lot of quick, light movements.

tread*
[tred]

n. 발판, 페달, 접촉면; 밟기, 걷기; v. 밟다, 걷다
The tread of a step or stair is its flat upper surface.

tip^{복습}
[tip]

① v. 뒤집(히)다; 기울이다 ② n. (뾰족한) 끝 ③ n. 팁, 사례금
If you tip an object or part of your body or if it tips, it moves into a sloping position with one end or side higher than the other.

grumble*
[grʌmbl]

v. 낮은 소리로 으르렁거리다; 투덜거리다, 불평하다; n. 투덜댐, 불평
If something grumbles, it makes a low continuous sound.

grind*
[graind]

v. 삐걱거리(게 하)다; 갈다, 찧다, 빻다; 비벼 문지르다
When something grinds, it makes a grating or grinding sound by rubbing together.

flee^{복습}
[fliː]

vi. (fled–fled) 달아나다, 도망치다; 사라지다
If you flee from something or someone, or flee a person or thing, you escape from them.

embarrass^{복습}
[embǽrəs]

v. 당황스럽게 만들다, 곤란하게 하다 (embarrassment n. 당황, 당혹)
If something or someone embarrasses you, they make you feel shy or ashamed.

drawer^{복습}
[drɔːr]

n. 서랍
A drawer is part of a desk, chest, or other piece of furniture that is shaped like a box and is designed for putting things in.

wiggle^{복습}
[wigl]

v. (몸을) 뒤흔들다, (좌우로) 움직이다; n. 뒤흔듦
If you wiggle something or if it wiggles, it moves up and down or from side to side in small quick movements.

awkward^{복습}
[ɔ́ːkwərd]

a. 어색한, 불편한, 곤란한 (awkwardly ad. 어색하게, 거북하게)
Someone who feels awkward behaves in a shy or embarrassed way.

marble*
[maːrbl]

n. 구슬, 구슬치기; 대리석
A marble is one of the small balls used in the game of marbles.

click*
[klik]

v. 찰칵[딸깍]하는 소리를 내다; n. 찰칵[딸깍](하는 소리)
If something clicks or if you click it, it makes a short, sharp sound.

particular^{복습}
[pərtíkjələr]

a. 특정한, 특별한, 특유의 (particularly ad. 특히, 두드러지게)
You use particular to emphasize that you are talking about one thing or one kind of thing rather than other similar ones.

charm[**]
[tʃɑːrm]

n. 작은 장식물; 매력; 마법 v. 매혹하다; 주문[마법]을 걸다
A charm is a small ornament that is fixed to a bracelet or necklace.

bracelet
[bréislit]

n. 팔찌
A bracelet is a chain or band, usually made of metal, which you wear around your wrist as jewelry.

chase[복습]
[tʃeis]

v. 뒤쫓다; 추구하다; 쫓아내다; n. 추적, 추격
If you chase someone, or chase after them, you run after them or follow them quickly in order to catch or reach them.

perimeter[*]
[pərímitər]

n. 둘레, 주변, 주위; 경계선
The perimeter of an area of land is the whole of its outer edge or boundary.

clue[*]
[kluː]

n. 단서, 실마리
A clue is a sign or some information which helps you to find the answer to a problem.

vivid[*]
[vívid]

a. (색·빛 등이) 선명한, 강렬한; 생생한, 발랄한
Something that is vivid is very bright in color.

glint[복습]
[glint]

v. 반짝이다, 빛나다; n. 반짝임, 섬광
If something glints, it produces or reflects a quick flash of light.

ember[복습]
[émbər]

n. (pl.) (꺼져가는 불 속의) 붉은 석탄[장작], 타다 남은 것
The embers of a fire are small pieces of wood or coal that remain and glow with heat after the fire has finished burning.

nursery[복습]
[nə́ːrsəri]

n. 육아실, 탁아소, 보육원; 양성소, 훈련소
A nursery is a place where children who are not old enough to go to school are looked after.

nod[복습]
[nɔd]

v. 끄덕이다, 끄덕여 표시하다; n. (동의·인사·신호·명령의) 끄덕임
If you nod, you move your head downward and upward to show agreement, understanding, or approval.

vanish[복습]
[vǽniʃ]

v. 사라지다, 없어지다, 모습을 감추다
If someone or something vanishes, they disappear suddenly or in a way that cannot be explained.

fumble
[fʌmbl]

vi. 손으로 더듬어 찾다; 우물우물 말하다
If you fumble for something or fumble with something, you try and reach for it or hold it in a clumsy way.

smooth[복습]
[smuːð]

a. 매끄러운; 유창한; v. 매끄럽게 하다, 반반하게 하다
You use smooth to describe something that is going well and is free of problems or trouble.

snatch[*]
[snætʃ]

v. 와락 붙잡다, 잡아채다; n. 잡아 뺏음, 강탈
If you snatch something or snatch at something, you take it or pull it away quickly.

dull[**]
[dʌl]

a. 둔한, 따분한, 재미없는; 흐릿한, 칙칙한 (dully ad. 멍청하게)
If you describe someone or something as dull, you mean they are not interesting or exciting.

flicker^{복습}
[flíkər]

v. (등불 · 희망 · 빛 등이) 깜박이다; n. 깜박임
If a light or flame flickers, it shines unsteadily.

indeed^{복습}
[indíd]

ad. 실로, 참으로, 과연, 정말
You use indeed to confirm or agree with something that has just been said.

uncover[*]
[ʌnkʌ́vər]

v. (비밀 등을) 알아내다[적발하다]; 덮개를 벗기다, 뚜껑을 열다
If you uncover something, especially something that has been kept secret, you discover or find out about it.

neat^{복습}
[ni:t]

a. 산뜻한, 깔끔한 (neatly ad. 깔끔하게)
A neat place, thing, or person is tidy and smart, and has everything in the correct place.

sting^{복습}
[stiŋ]

vt. (stung–stung) 찌르다, 쏘다; 따끔따끔하다; n. 찌름, 쏨
If something stings you, a sharp part of is pushed into your skin so that you feel a sharp pain.

blustery
[blʌ́stəri]

a. 날씨가 바람이 거센
Blustery weather is rough, windy, and often rainy, with the wind often changing in strength or direction.

vicious[*]
[víʃəs]

a. (날씨 · 고통 등이) 지독한, 격심한; 나쁜, 악덕의
A vicious person or a vicious blow is violent and cruel.

hallway^{복습}
[hɔ́:lwèi]

n. 복도; 현관
A hallway in a building is a long passage with doors into rooms on both sides of it.

gust
[gʌst]

n. 한바탕 부는 바람, 돌풍
A gust is a short, strong, sudden rush of wind.

invisible^{복습}
[invízəbl]

a. 보이지 않는, 볼 수 없는
If you describe something as invisible, you mean that it cannot be seen, for example because it is transparent, hidden, or very small.

needle^{복습}
[ni:dl]

n. 바늘, 침
A needle is a thin hollow metal rod with a sharp point.

whip[*]
[hwip]

v. 세차게 때리다; 채찍질하다; 홱 잡아채다; n. 채찍(질), 마부
If something, for example the wind, whips something, it strikes it sharply.

petulant
[pétʃulənt]

a. 안달하는, 심술 부리는, 성미 급한 (petulantly ad. 안달하여, 토라져)
Someone who is petulant is unreasonably angry and upset in a childish way.

leak[*]
[li:k]

v. 새(게 하)다; n. (물 · 공기 · 빛 등이) 새는 구멍
If a liquid or gas leaks, it comes out of a hole by accident.

impatient^{복습}
[impéiʃənt]

a. 성급한, 조급한, 참을성 없는 (impatiently ad. 성급하게, 조바심 내며)
If you are impatient, you are annoyed because you have to wait too long for something.

resist^{**}
[rizíst]

v. 저항하다, 반대하다, 방해하다
If you resist doing something, or resist the temptation to do it, you stop yourself from doing it although you would like to do it.

urge*
[əːrdʒ]

n. (강한) 충동; **v.** 촉구하다, 충고하다, 재촉하다
If you have an urge to do or have something, you have a strong wish to do or have it.

stride*
[straid]

n. 큰 걸음, 활보; **v.** 성큼성큼 걷다
A stride is a long step which you take when you are walking or running.

flat^{복습}
[flæt]

① **n.** (연립주택, 다세대 주택 등을 포함하는) 아파트식 주거지; 평지, 평원;
② **a.** 평평한, 균일한; 단호한
A flat is a set of rooms for living in, usually on one floor and part of a larger building. A flat usually includes a kitchen and bathroom.

random*
[rǽndəm]

a. 임의의, 무작위의 (randomly **ad.** 무작위로)
A random sample or method is one in which all the people or things involved have an equal chance of being chosen.

spell^{복습}
[spel]

v. 철자를 말하다; (낱말을) 맞춤법에 따라 쓰다; **n.** 주문(呪文), 주술; 마력, 마법
When you spell a word, you write or speak each letter in the word in the correct order.

jerk*
[dʒəːrk]

n. (갑자기) 홱 움직임; 반사 운동; **v.** 갑자기 움직이다
A jerk is a move with a sudden movement.

stumble^{복습}
[stʌmbl]

v. 비틀거리며 걷다, 발부리가 걸리다; **n.** 비틀거림
If you stumble, you put your foot down awkwardly while you are walking or running and nearly fall over.

cautious^{복습}
[kɔ́ːʃəs]

a. 조심성 있는, 신중한 (cautiously **ad.** 조심스럽게)
Someone who is cautious acts very carefully in order to avoid possible danger.

rustle^{복습}
[rʌsl]

vi. 바스락거리다, 살랑살랑 소리 내다; **n.** 바스락거리는 소리
If things such as paper or leaves rustle, or if you rustle them, they move about and make a soft, dry sound.

sweep^{복습}
[swiːp]

v. 휙 둘러보다, 휙 지나치다; 휩쓸어 가다, 쓸다; **n.** 한 번 휘두름; 청소
If something sweeps from one place to another, it moves there extremely quickly.

derelict
[dérəlikt]

a. (특히 대지나 건물이) 버려진, 이용되지 않는
A place or building that is derelict is empty and in a bad state of repair because it has not been used or lived in for a long time.

drape
[dreip]

vt. (우아하게) 걸치다, 주름을 잡아 예쁘게 덮다; **n.** 드리워진 모양, 드레이프
If you drape a piece of cloth somewhere, you place it there so that it hangs down in a casual and graceful way.

rot^{복습}
[rɑt]

v. 썩다, 썩이다; **n.** 썩음, 부패 (rotten **a.** 썩은; 형편없는, 끔찍한)
When food, wood, or another substance rots, or when something rots it, it becomes softer and is gradually destroyed.

decompose
[diːkəmpóuz]

v. (자연스런 화학 작용에 의해) 부패되다; (더 작은 부분들로) 분해하다
When things such as dead plants or animals decompose, or when something decomposes them, they change chemically and begin to decay.

jellyish
[dʒéliiʃ]

a. 젤리같은
Jellyish is resembling or characteristic of jelly.

bat^{복습}
[bæt]

① n. 박쥐 ② v. (배트 · 막대기로) 치다; n. (야구의) 배트, 막대기
A bat is a small flying animal that looks like a mouse with wings made of skin.

upside down
[ʌpsàid dáun]

ad. 거꾸로, 뒤집혀
If something has been moved upside down, it has been turned round so that the part that is usually lowest is above the part that is usually highest.

startle^{복습}
[staːrtl]

v. 깜짝 놀라게 하다; 움찔하다; n. 깜짝 놀람
If something sudden and unexpected startles you, it surprises and frightens you slightly.

whir
[hwəːr]

v. 윙 소리를 내며 날다; n. 윙 하는 소리
When something such as a machine or an insect's wing whirs, it makes a series of low sounds so quickly that they seem like one continuous sound.

duck
[dʌk]

① v. 피하다, 머리를 홱 숙이다 ② n. 오리
If you duck, you move your head or the top half of your body quickly downward to avoid something that might hit you, or to avoid being seen.

swoop
[swuːp]

v. 급강하하다, 내리 덮치다
When a bird or airplane swoops, it suddenly moves downward through the air in a smooth curving movement.

clamber
[klǽmbər]

vi. 기어 올라가다
If you clamber somewhere, you climb there with difficulty, usually using your hands as well as your feet.

scan[*]
[skæn]

v. 훑어 보다; 스캔하다; n. 정밀 검사; 스캔
When you scan a place or group of people, you look at it carefully, usually because you are looking for something or someone.

telltale
[téltèil]

a. 비밀을 폭로하는; 고자질하는; n. 고자질쟁이; 비밀을 폭로하는 것
Something that is described as telltale gives away information, often about something bad that would otherwise not be noticed.

ruin^{**}
[ruːin]

v. 망치다, 못쓰게 만들다; 몰락하다; n. 파멸, 멸망
To ruin something means to severely harm, damage, or spoil it.

scramble[*]
[skrǽmbl]

v. 기어오르다; 서로 (다투어) 빼앗다; 뒤섞다; n. 기어오르기
If you scramble over rocks or up a hill, you move quickly over them or up it using your hands to help you.

sac
[sæk]

n. (동식물 체내에서 액체 · 가스가 들어 있는) 주머니
A sac is a small part of an animal's body, shaped like a little bag. It contains air, liquid, or some other substance.

horrible^{**}
[hɔ́ːrəbl]

a. 끔찍한, 소름 끼치게 싫은; 무서운 (horribly a. 끔찍하게, 무섭게)
You can call something horrible when it causes you to feel great shock, fear, and disgust.

94

squash*
[skwɑʃ]

① v. 짓누르다, 으깨다 ② n. [식물] 호박
If someone or something is squashed, they are pressed or crushed with such force that they become injured or lose their shape.

press^{복습}
[pres]

v. 누르다, 밀어 누르다; 강요하다; n. 언론, 출판물; 누름, 압박
If you press something somewhere, you push it firmly against something else.

bleak*
[bli:k]

a. 황량한, 처량한, 삭막한
If you describe a place as bleak, you mean that it looks cold, empty, and unattractive.

damp^{복습}
[dæmp]

a. 축축한; n. 습기
Something that is damp is slightly wet.

disturb**
[distə́:rb]

v. 방해하다, 어지럽히다
If you disturb someone, you interrupt what they are doing and upset them.

pound^{복습}
[paund]

① v. 쿵쿵 울리다, 마구 치다, 세게 두드리다; n. 타격 ② n. 파운드(무게의 단위)
③ n. 울타리, 우리
If your heart is pounding, it is beating with an unusually strong and fast rhythm, usually because you are afraid.

chest^{복습}
[tʃest]

n. 가슴, 흉부; (나무로 만든) 궤, 상자
Your chest is the top part of the front of your body where your ribs, lungs, and heart are.

sticky*
[stíki]

a. 끈적[끈끈]한, 들러붙는, 점착성의
A sticky substance is soft, or thick and liquid, and can stick to other things.

cling*
[kliŋ]

vi. 매달리다, 달라붙다 (clinging a. 잘 들러붙는, 점착성의)
If you cling to someone or something, you hold onto them tightly.

stuff^{복습}
[stʌf]

n. 물건, 물질; vt. 채워 넣다, 속을 채우다
You can use stuff to refer to things such as a substance, a collection of things, events, or ideas, or the contents of something in a general way without mentioning the thing itself by name.

crackle
[krǽkl]

v. (불꽃 등이) 탁탁[치직] 소리를 내다; n. 딱딱[우지직] 하는 소리
If something crackles, it makes a rapid series of short, harsh noises.

cotton^{복습}
[katn]

n. 목화, 솜, 무명[실]; a. 면의, 무명의 (cotton candy n. 솜사탕)
Cotton candy is a large pink or white mass of sugar threads that is eaten from a stick. It is sold at fairs or other outdoor events.

slippery*
[slípəri]

a. 미끄러운, 미끈거리는
Something that is slippery is smooth, wet, or oily and is therefore difficult to walk on or to hold.

tug^{복습}
[tʌg]

v. (세게) 당기다, 끌다; 노력[분투]하다; n. 힘껏 당김; 분투, 노력
If you tug something or tug at it, you give it a quick and usually strong pull.

grasp*
[græsp]

n. 꽉 쥐기, 움켜잡기; v. 붙잡다, 움켜쥐다
A grasp is a very firm hold or grip.

loosen[*]
[lu:sn]

v. 풀다, 느슨해지다
If you loosen your grip on something, or if your grip loosens, you hold it less tightly.

relieve[복습]
[rilíːv]

vt. 안도하게 하다; (긴장·걱정 등을) 덜다 (relieved a. 안심한, 안도한)
If something relieves an unpleasant feeling or situation, it makes it less unpleasant or causes it to disappear completely.

shone[복습]
[ʃoun]

v. SHINE(빛나다, 비추다)의 과거·과거분사
Something that shines is very bright and clear because it is reflecting light.

resemble[*]
[rizémbl]

vt. ~을 닮다, ~와 공통점이 있다
If one thing or person resembles another, they are similar to each other.

lump[복습]
[lʌmp]

n. 덩어리, 한 조각; v. 한 덩어리로 만들다
A lump of something is a solid piece of it.

meld
[meld]

v. 섞이다, 혼합하다
To meld means to blend or become blended.

ghastly
[gǽstli]

a. 무시무시한, 지독한; 핏기 없는, 창백한; ad. 송장같이, 창백하여
If you describe someone or something as ghastly, you mean that you find them very unpleasant.

warn[복습]
[wɔːrn]

v. 경고하다; ~에게 통지[통고]하다 (warning n. 경고)
If you warn someone about something such as a possible danger or problem, you tell them about it so that they are aware of it.

grab[*]
[græb]

n. 부여잡기; v. 부여잡다, 움켜쥐다
A grab is an act or an instance of picking something up suddenly and roughly.

scrape[*]
[skreip]

v. 긁(어내)다, 벗겨내다, 떼다; n. 긁힌 상처, 찰과상; 긁기
If you scrape a part of your body, you accidentally rub it against something hard and rough, and damage it slightly.

wail
[weil]

v. (큰소리로) 투덜거리다; 울부짖다; n. 울부짖음, 한탄
If you wail something, you say it in a loud, high-pitched voice that shows that you are unhappy or in pain.

buzz[*]
[bʌz]

v. 윙윙거리다; 분주하게 돌아다니다; n. 윙윙거리는 소리
If something buzzes or buzzes somewhere, it makes a long continuous sound, like the noise a bee makes when it is flying.

windowpane[*]
[windoupèin]

n. 창유리
A windowpane is a piece of glass in the window of a building.

thief[**]
[θiːf]

n. 도둑, 절도범
A thief is a person who steals something from another person.

terrify[*]
[térəfài]

vt. 무섭게[겁나게] 하다
If something terrifies you, it makes you feel extremely frightened.

attach[*]
[ətǽtʃ]

vt. 붙이다, 부착하다 (attached a. 붙여진)
If you attach something to an object, you connect it or fasten it to the object.

96

encase
[inkéis]

vt. 싸다, (상자 등에) 넣다
If a person or an object is encased in something, they are completely covered or surrounded by it.

cocoon
[kəkú:n]

n. 안식처, 보호막; 누에고치
If you are in a cocoon of something, you are wrapped up in it or surrounded by it.

flap*
[flæp]

v. 펄럭이(게 하)다, 휘날리다, 퍼덕이다; n. 펄럭임, 퍼덕거림
If a bird or insect flaps its wings or if its wings flap, the wings move quickly up and down.

spot**
[spɑt]

vt. 발견하다, 분별하다; n. 장소, 지점; 반점, 얼룩
If you spot something or someone, you notice them.

chapter nine

1. The other mother claimed to love Coraline. How did Coraline describe the kind of love she showed?
   A. She loved Coraline as her own mother.
   B. She loved Coraline as a real daughter.
   C. She loved Coraline as a friend.
   D. She loved Coraline as a possession or pet.

2. Why did the other mother give Coraline the key to the flat?
   A. She wanted her to escape from the house.
   B. She wanted her to open the door to the empty flat.
   C. She wanted her to go bring her something from the room.
   D. She wanted her to fix it, because it was broken.

3. Why was the other father underneath the empty flat?
   A. He was being punished by the other mother for talking to Coraline.
   B. He was searching for the hidden souls before Coraline.
   C. He was hiding from the other mother and Coraline.
   D. He lived down there alone in the dark.

4. Why did Coraline feel pity for the creature in the basement?

    A. It was made by the other mother and then tossed aside.

    B. It was no longer able to move on its own.

    C. It was sick and lonely.

    D. It really wanted to hurt Coraline.

5. Why did the creature urge Coraline to leave the place?

    A. It wanted her to leave it alone in quiet peace.

    B. It was being pushed by the other mother to hurt Coraline.

    C. Coraline had already found the soul down there.

    D. The trapdoor was going to close and lock them both inside.

6. How did the creature lose its second button eye?

    A. It nodded its head too hard and shook the eye loose.

    B. It bumped into a wall and knocked its eye off.

    C. The ghost children helped Coraline rip it off.

    D. The button was torn off by Coraline.

7. How did the creature try to find Coraline after it lost its button eyes?

    A. It tried to hear her.

    B. It tried to smell her.

    C. It tried to feel around for her.

    D. It tried calling out to her.

$$\frac{2{,}230 \text{ words}}{\text{reading time (} \quad \text{) sec}} \times 60 = (\qquad) \text{ WPM}$$

Build Your Vocabulary

swirl
[swəːrl]

vi. 소용돌이치다, 빙빙 돌다
If liquid or flowing swirls, it moves round and round quickly.

mist^{※合}
[mist]

n. 안개; v. 안개가 끼다, 눈이 흐려지다
Mist consists of a large number of tiny drops of water in the air, which make it difficult to see very far.

crouch^{※合}
[krautʃ]

v. 몸을 쭈그리다, 쪼그리고 앉다; 웅크리다; n. 웅크림
If you are crouching, your legs are bent under you so that you are close to the ground and leaning forward slightly.

sticky^{※合}
[stíki]

a. 끈적[끈끈]한, 들러붙는, 점착성의
A sticky substance is soft, or thick and liquid, and can stick to other things.

stuff^{※合}
[stʌf]

n. 물건, 물질; vt. 채워 넣다, 속을 채우다
You can use stuff to refer to things such as a substance, a collection of things, events, or ideas, or the contents of something in a general way without mentioning the thing itself by name.

cling^{※合}
[klin]

vi. 매달리다, 달라붙다
If you cling to someone or something, you hold onto them tightly.

slant[*]
[slænt]

v. 기울(게 하)다, 경사지(게 하)다; a. 기울어진, 비스듬한; n. 경사, 비탈
Something that slants is sloping, rather than horizontal or vertical.

fury[*]
[fjúəri]

n. 격노, 격분; 격심함, 맹렬함
Fury is violent or very strong anger.

crook
[kruk]

v. 구부리다; 굽다; n. 갈고리; 악한, 사기꾼
If you crook your arm or finger, you bend it.

fog^{※合}
[fɔːg]

n. 안개; 혼란
When there is fog, there are tiny drops of water in the air which form a thick cloud and make it difficult to see things.

nod^{※合}
[nɔd]

v. 끄덕이다, 끄덕여 표시하다; n. (동의·인사·신호·명령의) 끄덕임
If you nod, you move your head downward and upward to show agreement, understanding, or approval.

miser
[máizər]

n. 구두쇠
If you say that someone is a miser, you disapprove of them because they seem to hate spending money, and to spend as little as possible.

100

possess**
[pəzés]

vt. 소유하다, 가지고 있다 (possession n. 소유, 소유물)
If you possess something, you have it or own it.

tolerate*
[tálərèit]

vt. 관대히 다루다, 묵인하다; 참다, 견디다
If you tolerate a situation or person, you accept them although you do not particularly like them.

amuse*
[əmjú:z]

vt. 즐겁게 하다, 재미나게 하다 (amusing a. 재미있는, 즐거운)
If something amuses you, it makes you want to laugh or smile.

ponder
[pándər]

v. 숙고하다, 깊이 생각하다
If you ponder something, you think about it carefully.

flatten*
[flǽtn]

vt. 평평하게 하다, 납작하게 하다
If you flatten something or if it flattens, it becomes flat or flatter.

drift복습
[drift]

v. 표류하다, 떠돌다; n. 표류; 경향, 추세
When something drifts somewhere, it is carried there by the movement of wind or water.

brass복습
[bræs]

n. 놋쇠, 황동
Brass is a yellow-colored metal made from copper and zinc.

toss복습
[tɔ:s]

v. 던지다, 내던지다
If you toss something somewhere, you throw it there lightly, often in a rather careless way.

damp복습
[dæmp]

a. 축축한; n. 습기
Something that is damp is slightly wet.

chill*
[tʃil]

a. 냉랭한, 차가운; v. 춥게 하다, 오싹하다; n. 냉기, 한기
Chill weather is cold and unpleasant.

shiver복습
[ʃívər]

v. (추위·공포로) 후들후들 떨다; 전율하다; n. 떨림, 전율
When you shiver, your body shakes slightly because you are cold or frightened.

whisper복습
[hwíspə:r]

v. 속삭이다
When you whisper, you say something very quietly.

swing복습
[swiŋ]

v. (swung–swung) 휙 돌리다, 회전시키다, 빙 돌다; 휘두르다, 흔들다; 매달리다
If something swings in a particular direction or if you swing it in that direction, it moves in that direction with a smooth, curving movement.

discolor
[diskʌlər]

v. 변색시키다, 빛깔이 바래다
If something discolors or if it is discolored by something else, its original color changes, so that it looks unattractive.

rectangle*
[réktæŋgl]

n. 직사각형 (rectangular a. 직사각형의, 직각의)
A rectangle is a four-sided shape whose corners are all ninety degree angles. Each side of a rectangle is the same length as the one opposite to it.

mote복습
[mout]

n. (아주 작은) 티끌
A mote is a tiny piece of a substance.

whistle[**] [hwisl]

v. 휘파람 불다; n. 휘파람; 호각
When you whistle or when you whistle a tune, you make a series of musical notes by forcing your breath out between your lips, or your teeth.

floorboard [flɔːrbɔːrd]

n. (pl.) 바닥 널, 바닥
Floorboards are the long pieces of wood that a wooden floor is made up of.

grim[*] [grim]

a. 험상스러운, 무서운; 엄한, 엄격한 (grimly ad. 험악하게)
If a person or their behavior is grim, they are very serious, usually because they are worried about something.

kneel[*] [niːl]

vi. (knelt–knelt) 무릎 꿇다
When you kneel, you bend your legs so that your knees are touching the ground.

tug [tʌg]

v. (세게) 당기다, 끌다; 노력[분투]하다; n. 힘껏 당김; 분투, 노력
If you tug something or tug at it, you give it a quick and usually strong pull.

stiff [stif]

a. 단단한, 뻣뻣한; 완강한, 완고한 (stiffly ad. 단단하게, 뻣뻣하게)
Something that is stiff is firm or does not bend easily.

hinge[*] [hindʒ]

v. 경첩을 달다; n. (문 · 뚜껑 등의) 경첩 (hinged a. 경첩이 달린)
Something that is hinged is joined to another thing, or joined together, by means of a hinge.

square [skweər]

n. 정사각형; 구역, 광장; a. 정직한, 공정한; 정사각형의
A square is a shape with four sides that are all the same length and four corners that are all right angles.

trapdoor [træpdɔːr]

n. (마루 · 지붕 · 천장 · 무대의) 치켜 올리는 뚜껑문
A trapdoor is a small horizontal door in a floor, a ceiling, or on a stage.

flick [flik]

vt. 가볍게 치다, 튀기다; n. 가볍게 치기
If you flick a switch, or flick an electrical appliance on or off, you press the switch sharply so that it moves into a different position and works the equipment.

bulb[*] [bʌlb]

n. 구, 전구
A bulb is the glass part of an electric lamp, which gives out light when electricity passes through it.

cellar [sélər]

n. 지하 저장실
A cellar is a room underneath a building, which is often used for storing things in.

acrid [ǽkrid]

a. (냄새나 맛이) 매캐한[콕 쏘는 듯한]
An acrid smell or taste is strong and sharp, and usually unpleasant.

tang [tæŋ]

n. 싸한[톡 쏘는 듯한] 맛[냄새]
A tang is a strong, sharp smell or taste.

sour[**] [sauər]

a. (맛이) 신, 시큼한; (특히 우유가) 상한; 기분이 언짢은, 시큰둥한
Something that is sour has a sharp, unpleasant taste like the taste of a lemon.

102

vinegar[vínigər]

n. 식초, 초
Vinegar is a sharp-tasting liquid, usually made from sour wine or malt, which is used to make things such as salad dressing.

rust[rʌst]

v. (금속 등이) 녹슬다, 부식하다; n. 녹
If metal rusts or something rusts it, it becomes covered with a brown substance when it contact with water.

click[klik]

v. 찰칵[딸깍]하는 소리를 내다; n. 찰칵[딸깍](하는 소리)
If something clicks or if you click it, it makes a short, sharp sound.

naked[néikid]

a. (가리개 등이) 벗겨진; 벌거벗은, 아무것도 걸치지 않은
You can describe an object as naked when it does not have its normal covering.

flake[fleik]

v. 엷은 조각으로 벗겨지다; 얇게 자르다; (눈이) 펄펄 내리다; n. 얇은 조각, 파편
If something such as paint flakes, small thin pieces of it come off.

crude[kruːd]

a. 거친, 투박한; 가공하지 않은, 천연 그대로의
If you describe an object that someone has made as crude, you mean that it has been made in a very simple way or from very simple parts.

rubbish[rʌ́biʃ]

n. 쓰레기, 폐물; 어리석은 짓
Rubbish consists of unwanted things or waste material such as used paper, empty tins and bottles, and waste food.

mildew[míldjùː]

v. 곰팡이가 생기다[생기게 하다]; n. 곰팡이
To mildew means to affect or become affected by a soft white fungus.

decay[dikéi]

v. 부패하다, 썩다; 쇠퇴하다; n. 부패, 부식
When something decays, it is gradually destroyed by a natural process.

heap[hiːp]

n. 더미, 쌓아올린 것; 덩어리
A heap of things is a pile of them, especially a pile arranged in a rather untidy way.

crunch[krʌntʃ]

v. (무엇을 으스러뜨리는 소리를 내며) 가다, 우두둑 깨물다[부수다]; n. 우두둑 부서지는 소리
If something crunches or if you crunch it, it makes a breaking or crushing noise, for example when you step on it.

stick out

phrasal v. 불쑥 나오다, 돌출하다
If something sticks out, it is further out than something else.

moldy[móuldi]

a. 곰팡이 난; 곰팡이 같은, 진부한
Something that is moldy is covered with mold.

reveal[rivíːl]

vt. 드러내다, 보이다, 나타내다
If you reveal something that has been out of sight, you uncover it so that people can see it.

dim[dim]

a. 흐릿한, 희미한, 어둑한; v. 어둑하게 하다, 흐려지다
Dim light is not bright.

pale[peil]

a. 창백한; 엷은, 연한; 희미한; v. 엷어지(게 하)다
If someone looks pale, their face looks a lighter color than usual, usually because they are ill, frightened, or shocked.

swollen^{**}
[swóulən]

a. 부어오른, 부푼
If a part of your body is swollen, it is larger and rounder than normal, usually as a result of injury or illness.

grub
[grʌb]

n. 땅벌레, 굼벵이; v. 개간하다; 땅을 파헤치다
A grub is a young insect which has just come out of an egg and looks like a short fat worm.

puff^{복습}
[pʌf]

v. 부풀어 오르다; (연기를) 내뿜다, 숨을 헐떡이다; n. 훅 불기, 숨, 입김
If you puff your cheeks, you make them larger and rounder by filling them with air.

revulsion
[rivʌlʃən]

n. 극도의 불쾌감, 혐오감
Someone's revulsion at something is the strong feeling of disgust or disapproval they have toward it.

strand
[strænd]

n. 가닥, 줄, 끈 줄, 끈 밧줄
A strand of something such as hair, wire, or thread is a single thin piece of it.

faint^{복습}
[feint]

a. 희미한, 어렴풋한; vi. 기절하다 (faintly ad. 희미하게, 어렴풋이)
A faint sound, color, mark, feeling, or quality has very little strength or intensity.

resemble^{복습}
[rizémbl]

vt. ~을 닮다, ~와 공통점이 있다
If one thing or person resembles another, they are similar to each other.

twig^{복습}
[twig]

n. 잔가지, 가는 가지 (twiglike a. 잔가지같은)
A twig is a very small thin branch that grows out from a main branch of a tree or bush.

indistinct^{복습}
[indistíŋkt]

a. (형상·기억 등이) 뚜렷하지 않은, 희미한
(indistinctly ad. 분간[식별]할 수 없을 정도로, 희미하게)
Something that is indistinct is unclear and difficult to see, hear, or recognize.

monstrous^{*}
[mánstrəs]

a. 기괴한, 괴물 같은; 극악무도한, 끔찍한
If you describe an unpleasant thing as monstrous, you mean that it is extremely large in size or extent.

miserable^{*}
[mízərəbl]

a. 불쌍한, 비참한, 지독한
If you describe something as monstrous, you mean that it is extremely frightening because it appears unnatural or ugly.

punish^{***}
[pʌniʃ]

v. 벌하다, 응징하다, 처벌하다 (punishment n. 벌, 처벌)
To punish someone means to make them suffer in some way because they have done something wrong.

hesitate^{복습}
[hézətèit]

v. 주저하다, 머뭇거리다, 망설이다
If you hesitate, you do not speak or act for a short time, usually because you are uncertain, embarrassed, or worried about what you are going to say or do.

out of sorts

idiom 기분이 언짢은
If you are out of sorts, you feel bad-tempered.

104

pat ^{복습}
[pæt]

① v. 쓰다듬다, 톡톡 가볍게 치다; n. 쓰다듬기
② n. (보통 납작하고 네모진) 작은 덩어리
If you pat something or someone, you tap them lightly, usually with your hand held flat.

tacky
[tǽki]

a. (마르지 않아서) 들러붙는, 끈적끈적한
If something such as paint or glue is tacky, it is slightly sticky and not yet dry.

vigorous *
[vígərəs]

a. 강한, 힘찬; 원기 왕성한, 활발한 (vigorously ad. 힘차게)
A vigorous person does things with great energy and enthusiasm.

clatter *
[klǽtər]

v. 달그락거리며 가다, 달가닥달가닥 울리다; n. 달가닥하는 소리
If you say that people or things clatter somewhere, you mean that they move there noisily.

concrete *
[kánkri:t]

n. 콘크리트; a. 유형의, 구체적인
Concrete is a substance used for building which is made by mixing together cement, sand, small stones, and water.

vacant *
[véikənt]

a. 멍한, 공허한; 빈, 비어있는 (vacantly ad. 공허하게, 멍하게)
A vacant look or expression is one that suggests that someone does not understand something or that they are not thinking about anything in particular.

urgent ^{복습}
[ə́:rdʒənt]

a. 긴급한, 절박한
If something is urgent, it needs to be dealt with as soon as possible.

lunge
[lʌndʒ]

v. 돌진하다, 달려들다; n. 돌입, 돌진
If you lunge in a particular direction, you move in that direction suddenly and clumsily.

react *
[riǽkt]

v. 반응하다, 반응을 보이다
When you react to something that has happened to you, you behave in a particular way because of it.

chase ^{복습}
[tʃeis]

v. 뒤쫓다; 추구하다; 쫓아내다; n. 추적, 추격
If you chase someone, or chase after them, you run after them or follow them quickly in order to catch or reach them.

blind ^{복습}
[blaind]

a. 맹목적인; 눈먼, 장님의; v. (잠시) 앞이 안보이게 만들다; 눈이 멀게하다
(blindly ad. 마구잡이로)
If you say that someone is blind to a fact or a situation, you mean that they ignore it or are unaware of it, although you think that they should take notice of it or be aware of it.

horrible ^{복습}
[hɔ́:rəbl]

a. 끔찍한, 소름 끼치게 싫은; 무서운 (horribly a. 끔찍하게, 무섭게)
You can call something horrible when it causes you to feel great shock, fear, and disgust.

roar *
[rɔ:r]

vi. (큰 짐승 등이) 으르렁거리다, 고함치다; n. 외치는 소리; 으르렁거리는 소리
If someone roars, they shout something in a very loud voice.

frustrate *
[frʌstreit]

v. 좌절시키다, 꺾다; 방해하다 (frustration n. 좌절, 낙담)
If something frustrates you, it upsets or angers you because you are unable to do anything about the problems it creates.

rush**
[rʌʃ]

n. 돌진, 급습; 혼잡, 쇄도; v. 서두르다, 돌진하다 (in a rush idiom 아주 바쁘게)
A rush is a situation in which you need to go somewhere or do something very quickly.

sweep^{복습}
[swi:p]

v. (swept-swept) 휙 지나치다, 휙 둘러보다; 휩쓸어 가다, 쓸다;
n. 한 번 휘두름; 청소
If something sweeps from one place to another, it moves there extremely quickly.

tiptoe
[típtòu]

vi. 발끝으로 걷다, 발돋움하다; n. 발끝
If you tiptoe somewhere, you walk there very quietly without putting your heels on the floor when you walk.

flop
[flɑp]

v. 펄썩[털썩] 쓰러지다; 퍼덕거리다; n. 펄썩[털썩] 떨어짐
If something flops onto something else, it falls there heavily or untidily.

writhe^{복습}
[raið]

v. 몸부림치다, 몸을 뒤틀다; n. 몸부림, 뒹굴기; 고뇌
If you writhe, your body twists and turns violently backward and forward, usually because you are in great pain or discomfort.

sway*
[swei]

v. 흔들(리)다, 동요하다; 설득하다; n. 동요, 지배
When people or things sway, they lean or swing slowly from one side to the other.

gather^{복습}
[gǽðər]

v. 모으다, 모이다
When you gather something such as your strength, courage, or thoughts, you make an effort to prepare yourself to do something.

wit*
[wit]

n. 지혜, 분별력, 기지, 재치
Wit is the ability to use words or ideas in an amusing, clever, and imaginative way.

serpent^{복습}
[sə́:rpənt]

n. (특히 큰) 뱀
A serpent is a snake.

slither
[slíðər]

v. 주르르 미끄러지다; 주르르 미끄러짐
If you slither somewhere, you slide along in an uneven way

crash**
[kræʃ]

vt. 충돌하다, 추락하다; n. 쿵, 와르르 하는 소리; 충돌, 추락
If something crashes somewhere, it moves and hits something else violently, making a loud noise.

thump^{복습}
[θʌmp]

n. 탁[쿵] 하는 소리; 때림, 세게 쥐어박음; v. 부딪치다
A thump is a loud, dull sound by hitting something.

bang*
[bæŋ]

v. 부딪치다, 탕 치다, 쾅 닫(히)다; n. 쾅 하는 소리
If you bang on something or if you bang it, you hit it hard, making a loud noise.

rattle*
[rætl]

v. 왈각달각 소리 나다, 덜걱덜걱 움직이다; n. 덜거덕거리는 소리
When something rattles or when you rattle it, it makes short sharp knocking sounds because it is being shaken or it keeps hitting against something hard.

drive***
[draiv]

n. (주택의) 진입로; 자동차 여행; v. 운전하다; 몰아가다
A drive is a wide piece of hard ground, or sometimes a private road, that leads from the road to a person's house.

106

chapter ten

1. How did the flat of the other old man's house smell to Coraline?
   A. It smelled like a dead insect.
   B. It smelled like many rats lived within the room.
   C. It smelled like exotic foods like spices and fresh herbs.
   D. It smelled like exotic foods that had gone rotten.

2. What important thing did Coraline realize about the nature of the objects in the other world?
   A. The things would eventually turn back into the real objects.
   B. The other mother couldn't create things but only change those that already existed.
   C. The things had all been lost and abandoned in the other world.
   D. The other mother bought everything and put it there herself.

3. Which of the following is NOT a way in which the other old man told Coraline that other world will be better?
   A. There will never be boring days.
   B. Coraline will always eat delicious meals.
   C. Coraline can wear gloves and boots.
   D. The world will be the exact same everyday.

4. What suddenly happened to the other old man as Coraline got closer to him?
   A. He fell apart and rats fled away from his clothing.
   B. He sprang to life and attacked Coraline.
   C. He collapsed into a pile of dust.
   D. He turned into rats which then bit Coraline.

5. How did the way Coraline feel after falling from her bike differ from how she felt falling on the stairs?
   A. She felt embarrassed falling off of her bike, but she felt worried falling down the stairs.
   B. She felt a sense of pride falling off of her bike, but she felt angry falling down the stairs.
   C. She felt a sense of achievement falling off of her bike, but she felt nothing but loss falling down the stairs.
   D. She felt confused falling off of her bike, but she felt sad falling down the stairs.

6. How did the cat help Coraline obtain the final marble?
   A. It smelled the rat and told Coraline where to look for it.
   B. It held the rat down so that Coraline could take the marble from it.
   C. It caught and killed the rat that had taken the marble.
   D. It found the rat and trapped it in a corner for Coraline to catch.

7. Why is the cat suddenly got worried?
   A. The other mother was about to attack Coraline.
   B. The ways in and out of the other world had disappeared.
   C. It was afraid of things waiting in the mist.
   D. Coraline was too injured to face the other mother.

1분에 몇 단어를 읽는지 리딩 속도를 측정해보세요.

$$\frac{2,354 \text{ words}}{\text{reading time ( ) sec}} \times 60 = (\quad) \text{ WPM}$$

Build Your Vocabulary

topmost
[tápmòust]

a. (위치 · 지위 등이) 최고의, 최상(급)의
The topmost thing in a number of things is the one that is highest or nearest the top.

flat^{복습}
[flæt]

① n. (연립주택, 다세대 주택 등을 포함하는) 아파트식 주거지
② a. 평평한, 균일한; 단호한; n. 평지, 평원
A flat is a set of rooms for living in, usually on one floor and part of a larger building. A flat usually includes a kitchen and bathroom.

charity*
[ʧǽrəti]

n. 자비, 자선, 자애
If you do something for charity, you do it in order to raise money for one or more charitable organizations.

doorway^{복습}
[dɔ́:rwèi]

n. 문간, 현관, 출입구
A doorway is a space in a wall where a door opens and closes.

mustache^{복습}
[mʌ́stæʃ]

n. 코밑수염
A man's mustache is the hair that grows on his upper lip.

envelope*
[énvəlòup]

n. 봉투, 봉지
An envelope is the rectangular paper cover in which you send a letter to someone through the post.

odd**
[ɑd]

a. 이상한, 기묘한
If you describe someone or something as odd, you think that they are strange or unusual.

cheesy
[ʧí:zi]

a. 치즈 냄새[맛]가 나는; 싸구려의, 저급한
Cheesy food is food that tastes or smells of cheese.

explorer^{복습}
[iksplɔ́:rər]

n. 탐험가; 조사자, 검사자
An explorer is someone who travels to places about which very little is known, in order to discover what is there.

muffle
[mʌ́fl]

vt. (소리를) 죽이다, 억제하다; 덮다, 싸다; n. 덮개
(muffled a. 소리가 우물거리는, 알아듣기 어려운)
If something muffles a sound, it makes the sound quieter and more difficult to hear.

mist^{복습}
[mist]

n. 안개; v. 안개가 끼다, 눈이 흐려지다 (misty a. 안개가 자욱한, 안개로 쌓인)
Mist consists of a large number of tiny drops of water in the air, which make it difficult to see very far.

cellar^{복습}
[sélər]

n. 지하 저장실
A cellar is a room underneath a building, which is often used for storing things in.

attic^{복습}
[ǽtik]

n. 다락(방), 지붕밑 방
An attic is a room at the top of a house just below the roof.

swing^{복습}
[swiŋ]

v. (swung-swung) 휙 돌리다, 회전시키다, 빙 돌다; 휘두르다, 흔들다; 매달리다
If something swings in a particular direction or if you swing it in that direction, it moves in that direction with a smooth, curving movement.

nerve**
[nəːrv]

n. 신경 (조직); 용기; v. 용기를 내어 ~하게 하다
Nerves are long thin fibers that transmit messages between your brain and other parts of your body.

deserve***
[dizə́ːrv]

vt. ~을 할[받을] 만하다, ~할 가치가 있다
If you say that a person or thing deserves something, you mean that they should have it or receive it because of their actions or qualities.

scurry^{복습}
[skə́ːri]

vi. 종종걸음으로 달리다, 급히 가다
When people or small animals scurry somewhere, they move there quickly and hurriedly, especially because they are frightened.

slip^{복습}
[slip]

v. 살짝 들어가다[나오다]; 미끄러지다; 슬며시 두다
If you slip somewhere, you go there quickly and quietly.

edge^{복습}
[edʒ]

n. 가장자리, 변두리, 끝; v. 조금씩[살살] 움직이다[이동시키다]; 테두리를 두르다
The edge of something is the place or line where it stops, or the part of it that is furthest from the middle.

exotic^{복습}
[igzátik]

a. 외래의, 외국의, 이국풍의
Something that is exotic is unusual and interesting, usually because it comes from a distant country.

rot^{복습}
[rat]

v. 썩다, 썩이다; n. 썩음, 부패 (rotten a. 썩은)
When food, wood, or another substance rots, or when something rots it, it becomes softer and is gradually destroyed.

rustle^{복습}
[rʌsl]

vi. 바스락거리다, 살랑살랑 소리 내다; n. 바스락거리는 소리
(rustling a. 와삭와삭[바스락바스락] 소리 나는, 옷 스치는 소리가 나는)
If things such as paper or leaves rustle, or if you rustle them, they move about and make a soft, dry sound.

frighten^{복습}
[fraitn]

v. 놀라게 하다, 섬뜩하게 하다; 기겁하다 (frightened a. 겁먹은)
If something or someone frightens you, they cause you to suddenly feel afraid, anxious, or nervous.

illusion^{복습}
[ilúːʒən]

n. 환영, 환각, 착각
An illusion is something that appears to exist or be a particular thing but does not actually exist or is in reality something else.

ghastly^{복습}
[gǽstli]

a. 무시무시한, 지독한; 핏기 없는, 창백한; ad. 송장같이, 창백하여
If you describe someone or something as ghastly, you mean that you find them very unpleasant.

parody^{복습}
[pǽrədi]

n. 패러디 (다른 것을 풍자적으로 모방한 글 · 음악 · 연극 등); (형편없는) 놀림감;
v. 패러디하다
When you say that something is a parody of a particular thing, you are criticizing it because you think it is a very poor example or bad imitation of that thing.

corridor^{복습}
[kɔ́:ridər]

n. 복도
A corridor is a long passage in a building or train, with doors and rooms on one or both sides.

distort^{복습}
[distɔ́:rt]

vt. 비틀다; 왜곡하다; (얼굴 등을) 찡그리다, 찌푸리다
If something you can see or hear is distorted or distorts, its appearance or sound is changed so that it seems unclear.

wonder^{복습}
[wʌ́ndə:r]

v. 호기심을 가지다, 이상하게 여기다; n. 경탄할 만한 것, 경이
If you wonder about something, you think about it, either because it interests you and you want to know more about it, or because you are worried or suspicious about it.

mantelpiece^{복습}
[mǽntlpìːs]

n. 벽난로 위 선반
A mantelpiece is a wood or stone shelf which is the top part of a border round a fireplace.

bare^{복습}
[bɛər]

a. 텅 빈; 있는 그대로의; 벌거벗은; v. 드러내다
If a room, cupboard, or shelf is bare, it is empty.

train^{복습}
[trein]

① n. 연속, 과정 ② n. 기차, 열차
③ v. (총 · 카메라 등을) 겨누다, 조준하다; 훈련하다, 연습하다
A train of thought or a train of events is a connected sequence, in which each thought or event seems to occur naturally or logically as a result of the previous one.

interrupt**
[intərʌ́pt]

v. 방해하다, 가로막다, 저지하다
If you interrupt someone who is speaking, you say or do something that causes them to stop.

scratch^{복습}
[skrætʃ]

v. 긁다, 할퀴다; n. 할큄, 찰과상 (scratchy a. (펜 따위가) 긁히는 소리를 내는)
If you scratch yourself, you rub your fingernails against your skin because it is itching.

enormous^{복습}
[inɔ́:rməs]

a. 엄청난, 거대한, 막대한
You can use enormous to emphasize the great degree or extent of something.

slant^{복습}
[slænt]

v. 기울(게 하)다, 경사지(게 하)다; a. 기울어진, 비스듬한; n. 경사, 비탈
(slanting a. 경사진, 기운)
Something that slants is sloping, rather than horizontal or vertical.

bundle^{복습}
(someone) up

phrasal v. ~을 따뜻하게 둘러싸다
If you bundle someone up, you make them feel warmer by putting warm clothes on them or covering them with blankets.

pavement*
[péivmənt]

n. 포장 도로
A pavement is a path with a hard surface, usually by the side of a road.

swear^{복습}
[swɛər]

v. (swore–sworn) 맹세하다, 단언하다; 욕을 하다; n. 맹세, 선서
If you swear to do something, you promise in a serious way that you will do it.

ignore^{복습}
[ignɔ́:r]

vt. 무시하다, 모르는 체하다
If you ignore someone or something, you pay no attention to them.

figure^{복습}
[fígjər]

n. 모습, 인물; 숫자, 계산; 도형, 도표; v. 계산하다; 생각하다, 판단하다
You refer to someone that you can see as a figure when you cannot see them clearly or when you are describing them.

drag^{복습}
[dræg]

v. 끌다, 힘들게 움직이다; n. 견인, 끌기
If you drag something, you pull it along the ground.

awful^{복습}
[ɔ́:fəl]

a. 몹시 나쁜, 지독한; 엄청, 굉장한; ad. 몹시
If you say that something is awful, you mean that it is extremely unpleasant, shocking, or bad.

recipe^{복습}
[résəpi:]

n. (요리의) 조리법; (약제 등의) 처방전
A recipe is a list of ingredients and a set of instructions that tell you how to cook something.

entire^{복습}
[intáiər]

a. 전체의; 완전한 (entirely ad. 완전히, 전적으로)
You use entire when you want to emphasize that you are referring to the whole of something, for example, the whole of a place, time, or population.

rhino^{복습}
[ráinou]

n. (= rhinoceros) 코뿔소
A rhino is a large Asian or African animal with thick gray skin and a horn, or two horns, on its nose.

octopus[*]
[áktəpəs]

n. 문어
An octopus is a soft sea creature with eight long arms called tentacles which it uses to catch food.

chest^{복습}
[tʃest]

n. 가슴, 흉부; (나무로 만든) 궤, 상자
Your chest is the top part of the front of your body where your ribs, lungs, and heart are.

height^{**}
[hait]

n. 높이; (사람의) 키, 신장
Height is the quality of being tall.

twinkle^{복습}
[twiŋkl]

v. 반짝반짝 빛나다; 깜빡이다; n. 반짝거림
If a star or a light twinkles, it shines with an unsteady light which rapidly and constantly changes from bright to faint.

shone^{복습}
[ʃoun]

v. SHINE(빛나다, 비추다)의 과거·과거분사
Something that shines is very bright and clear because it is reflecting light.

stick^{복습}
[stik]

① n. 막대기, 지팡이 ② v. 찔러 넣다, 찌르다; 붙이다, 달라붙다; 꽂히다, 박히다
A stick is a long thin piece of wood which is used for a particular purpose.

poke^{복습}
[pouk]

v. 찌르다, 쑤시다; n. 찌름, 쑤심
If you poke someone or something, you quickly push them with your finger or with a sharp object.

chapter ten

113

fall apart^{복습}

phrasal v. 무너지다, 산산조각나다
If something falls apart, it breaks owing to long use or poor construction.

leap^{복습}
[li:p]

v. (leapt/leaped–leapt/leaped) 껑충 뛰다, 뛰어넘다; n. 뜀, 도약
If you leap, you jump high in the air or jump a long distance.

sleeve[*]
[sli:v]

n. (옷의) 소매, 소맷자락
The sleeves of a coat, shirt, or other item of clothing are the parts that cover your arms.

score^{**}
[skɔ:r]

n. 20, 스무 개 정도; 득점, 점수; vi. 득점을 매기다, 기록하다
A score is twenty or approximately twenty.

chitter^{복습}
[tʃítər]

v. 지저귀다; (추워서) 떨다
To chitter means to twitter or chirp.

flee^{복습}
[fli:]

vi. (fled–fled) 달아나다, 도망치다; 사라지다
If you flee from something or someone, or flee a person or thing, you escape from them.

flutter^{복습}
[flʌtə:r]

v. (깃발 등이) 펄럭이다, (새 등이) 날갯짓하다; n. 펄럭임
If something thin or light flutters, or if you flutter it, it moves up and down or from side to side with a lot of quick, light movements.

greasy
[grí:si]

a. 기름진, 기름투성이의
Something that is greasy has a thick, oily substance on it or in it.

marble^{복습}
[ma:rbl]

n. 구슬, 구슬치기; 대리석
A marble is one of the small balls used in the game of marbles.

scan^{복습}
[skæn]

v. 훑어 보다; 스캔하다; n. 정밀 검사; 스캔
When you scan a place or group of people, you look at it carefully, usually because you are looking for something or someone.

squint[*]
[skwint]

v. 실눈으로 보다, 곁눈질을 하다; a. 사시의; 곁눈질하는
If you squint at something, you look at it with your eyes partly closed.

forepaw
[fɔ:rpɔ:]

n. (개 · 고양이 등의) 앞발
Forepaw means either of the front feet of most land mammals that do not have hoofs.

determine[*]
[ditə́:rmin]

v. 결심하다, 결정하다 (determined a. 결연한, 단호한)
If you are determined to do something, you have made a firm decision to do it and will not let anything stop you.

distract[*]
[distrǽkt]

vt. (마음 · 주의를) 흐트러뜨리다, 딴 데로 돌리다
If something distracts you or your attention from something, it takes your attention away from it.

observe^{***}
[əbzə́:rv]

vt. 관찰하다, 목격하다
If you observe a person or thing, you watch them carefully, especially in order to learn something about them.

distinct^{***}
[distíŋkt]

a. 뚜렷한, 명백한; 별개의, 다른
If something is distinct, you can hear, see, or taste it clearly.

flatten^{복습}
[flǽtn]

vt. 평평하게 하다, 납작하게 하다
If you flatten something or if it flattens, it becomes flat or flatter.

remind^{복습}
[rimáind]

vt. 생각나게 하다, 상기시키다, 일깨우다
If someone reminds you of a fact or event that you already know about, they say something which makes you think about it.

pell-mell
[pel-mel]

ad. 허둥지둥, 황급히
If you move pell-mell somewhere, you move there in a hurried, uncontrolled way.

pursuit[*]
[pərsú:t]

n. 추적, 추격; 추구 (in pursuit of idiom ~을 추적 중이다)
Someone who is in pursuit of a person, vehicle, or animal is chasing them.

gain on

phrasal v. (쫓고 있는) ~에 점점 가까워지다
If you are gaining on someone or something, you are getting closer to them, especially when you are chasing.

flight^{**}
[flait]

n. (계단의 방향이 변하지 않는) 일련, 연속; 비행
A flight of steps or stairs is a set of steps or stairs that lead from one level to another without changing direction.

skid
[skid]

v. 미끄러지다; n. 미끄럼, 옆으로 미끄러짐
If a vehicle skids, it slides sideways or forward while moving, for example when you are trying to stop it suddenly on a wet road.

crash^{복습}
[kræʃ]

vt. 충돌하다, 추락하다; n. 쿵, 와르르 하는 소리; 충돌, 추락
If something crashes somewhere, it moves and hits something else violently, making a loud noise.

concrete^{복습}
[kánkri:t]

n. 콘크리트; a. 유형의, 구체적인
Concrete is a substance used for building which is made by mixing together cement, sand, small stones, and water.

scrape^{복습}
[skreip]

v. 긁(어내)다, 벗겨내다, 떼다; n. 긁힌 상처, 찰과상; 긁기
If you scrape something from a surface, you remove it, especially by pulling a sharp object over the surface.

skin^{**}
[skin]

v. (피부가) 까지다; 껍질을 벗기다; n. 피부; 가죽
If one's knee or elbow is skinned, it is injured by scraping.

mess^{복습}
[mes]

n. 엉망진창, 난잡함; v. 망쳐놓다, 방해하다
If you say that something is a mess or in a mess, you think that it is in an untidy state.

grit^{복습}
[grit]

n. 티끌, 먼지, 모래; v. 이를 갈다, 쓸리다, 삐걱삐걱 (소리 나게) 하다
Grit is very small particles of a hard material, especially of stone or sand.

sting^{복습}
[stiŋ]

vt. (stung-stung) 따끔따끔하다; 찌르다, 쏘다; n. 찌름, 쏨
If a part of your body stings, or if a substance stings it, you feel a sharp pain there.

trickle
[trikl]

vi. 똑똑 떨어지다, 졸졸 흐르다; n. 물방울, 실개울
If liquid trickles somewhere, it flows slowly and without force in a thin line.

rip*
[rip]

v. 찢다, 벗겨내다; n. 찢어진 틈, 잡아 찢음 (ripped a. 찢어진)
When something rips or when you rip it, you tear it forcefully with your hands or with a tool such as a knife.

scab
[skæb]

n. (상처의) 딱지; v. 딱지가 생기다
A scab is a hard, dry covering that forms over the surface of a wound.

swallow**
[swálou]

v. 삼키다, 목구멍으로 넘기다; (초조해서) 마른침을 삼키다
If you swallow something, you cause it to go from your mouth down into your stomach.

lie^{복습}
[lai]

vi. 눕다, 누워 있다; 놓여 있다, 위치하다
If you are lying somewhere, you are in a horizontal position and are not standing or sitting.

whisker^{복습}
[wískəːr]

n. (고양이 · 쥐 등의) 수염; 구레나룻
The whiskers of an animal such as a cat or a mouse are the long stiff hairs that grow near its mouth.

stiff^{복습}
[stif]

a. 단단한, 뻣뻣한; 완강한, 완고한
Something that is stiff is firm or does not bend easily.

visible*
[vízəbl]

a. 눈에 보이는, 명백한
You use visible to describe something or someone that people notice or recognize.

collar**
[kálər]

n. (개 등의) 목걸이; 칼라, 깃; vt. 깃을 달다
A collar is a band of leather or plastic which is put round the neck of a dog or cat.

glisten
[glisn]

vi. 반짝이다, 반짝반짝 빛나다; n. 반짝임
If something glistens, it shines, usually because it is wet or oily.

decapitate
[dikǽpitèit]

v. 목을 자르다, 참수하다 (decapitated a. 목이 잘린)
If someone is decapitated, their head is cut off.

smug
[smʌg]

a. 잘난 체하는, 점잖은 체하는
If you say that someone is smug, you are criticizing the fact they seem very pleased with how good, clever, or lucky they are.

expression^{복습}
[ikspréʃən]

n. 표정, 표현, 표현법
Your expression is the way that your face looks at a particular moment. It shows what you are thinking or feeling

at the best^{복습}
of times

idiom (보통 부정문에서) 가장 좋은 때[상황, 상태]에도
You say at the best of times when you are making a negative or critical comment to emphasize that it is true even when the circumstances are as favorable as possible.

urgent^{복습}
[ə́ːrdʒənt]

a. 긴급한, 절박한 (urgently ad. 긴박하게)
If something is urgent, it needs to be dealt with as soon as possible.

prickle
[prikl]

v. 뜨끔뜨끔 쑤시다; 찌르다; n. 찌르는 듯한 아픔; 가시, 바늘
If your skin prickles, it feels as if a lot of small sharp points are being stuck into it, either because of something touching it or because you feel a strong emotion.

transform[*]
[trænsfɔ́ːrm]

v. 변형시키다, 변형하다; n. 변형
To transform something into something else means to change or convert it into that thing.

admit[복습]
[ədmít]

v. 인정하다
If you admit that something bad, unpleasant, or embarrassing is true, you agree, often unwillingly, that it is true.

guarantee[복습]
[gæ̀rəntíː]

n. 보증, 개런티; vt. 보증하다, 다짐하다
Something that is a guarantee of something else makes it certain that it will happen or that it is true.

crude[복습]
[kruːd]

a. 거친, 투박한; 가공하지 않은, 천연 그대로의
If you describe an object that someone has made as crude, you mean that it has been made in a very simple way or from very simple parts.

charcoal
[ʧɑ́ːrkòul]

n. 숯, 목탄
Charcoal is a black substance obtained by burning wood without much air. It can be burned as a fuel, and small sticks of it are used for drawing with.

scribble
[skríbl]

n. 낙서; v. 갈겨쓰다, 날려 쓰다; 낙서하다
Scribble is something that has been written or drawn quickly and roughly.

bristle[복습]
[brísl]

v. (털 등을) 곤두세우다; (화·용기 등을) 불러 일으키다 (bristling a. 곤두서있는)
If animal's fur bristles, it rises up as in fear.

chimney[*]
[ʧímni]

n. 굴뚝
A chimney is a pipe through which smoke goes up into the air, usually through the roof of a building.

sweep[복습]
[swiːp]

n. 청소; 한 번 휘두름; v. 휩쓸어 가다, 쓸다; 휙 둘러보다, 휙 지나치다
If you sweep an area of floor or ground, you push dirt or rubbish off it using a brush with a long handle.

swish
[swiʃ]

v. 휘두르다, 튀기다; 휙 소리 내다; n. 휙 소리
If something swishes or if you swish it, it moves quickly through the air, making a soft sound.

growl[*]
[graul]

v. 으르렁거리다, 고함치다; n. 으르렁거리는 소리
When a dog or other animal growls, it makes a low noise in its throat, usually because it is angry.

stroke[복습]
[strouk]

① vt. 쓰다듬다, 어루만지다; n. 쓰다듬기, 달램 ② n. 타격, 일격, 치기
If you stroke someone or something, you move your hand slowly and gently over them.

beat[복습]
[biːt]

v. (심장이) 고동치다; 치다, 두드리다; (날개를) 퍼덕거리다;
n. [음악] 박자, 고동; 퍼덕임
When your heart or pulse beats, it continually makes regular rhythmic movements.

tremble[복습]
[trémbl]

v. 떨다, 떨리다
If you tremble, you shake slightly because you are frightened or cold.

miserable^{복습}
[mízərəbl]

a. 불쌍한, 비참한, 지독한
If you describe a place or situation as miserable, you mean that it makes you feel unhappy or depressed.

resist^{복습}
[rizíst]

v. 저항하다, 반대하다, 방해하다
If you resist doing something, or resist the temptation to do it, you stop yourself from doing it although you would like to do it.

well^{복습}
[wel]

v. 솟아 나오다, 내뿜다, 분출하다; n. 우물
If liquids, for example tears, well, they come to the surface and form a pool.

aware**
[əwéər]

a. 알고 있는, 의식하고 있는, 알아차린
If you are aware of something, you realize that it is present or is happening because you hear it, see it, smell it, or feel it.

press^{복습}
[pres]

v. 누르다, 밀어 누르다; 강요하다; n. 언론, 출판물; 누름, 압박
If you press something somewhere, you push it firmly against something else.

scrawl
[skrɔːl]

n. 휘갈겨 쓰기[쓴 글씨]; vt. 휘갈겨 쓰다, 낙서하다
You can refer to writing that looks careless and untidy as a scrawl.

scatter^{복습}
[skǽtər]

v. 흩뿌리다, 뿌리다; 뿔뿔이 흩어지다 (scattering n. 소량, 흩어진 것)
A scattering of things or people is a small number of them spread over an area.

118

chapter eleven

1. The other mother described the cat as _____, but Coraline described it as _____.
   A. a liar; vermin
   B. a pest; a teddy bear
   C. vermin; a friend
   D. a pest; a protector

2. In regards to the other mother's altered appearance, why did Coraline find it to be funny?
   A. The other mother had put on more makeup to appear more attractive.
   B. The other mother looked nothing like her real mother.
   C. The other mother's hair was actually alive.
   D. The other mother looked almost exactly like her real mother.

3. Why did Coraline say that she knew her parents were in the passageway?
   A. She knew the passageway was her only way out, but she needed the other mother to open it.
   B. She actually believed that her parents were in fact in the passageway.
   C. She knew help was waiting for her on the other side of the door.
   D. She wanted to continue playing the game longer, because she enjoyed it.

4. How did Coraline catch the other mother off guard after she opened the door to the corridor?

   A. She threw the cat at the other mother's head.

   B. She pushed her into the corridor from behind.

   C. She surprised the other mother with the help of the ghost children.

   D. She threw the stone with the hole in it at the other mother.

5. How did Coraline finally manage to close the door?

   A. The door suddenly grew smaller and lighter.

   B. The other mother stopped resisting against the door.

   C. The cat bit the other mother's hand and the hand pulled back inside.

   D. The children and her parents' ghostly forms offered help to close the door.

6. Which of the following is NOT a way in which Coraline described the corridor?

   A. The walls felt warm to the touch.

   B. The corridor was getting smaller around her.

   C. The walls moved as if they were alive.

   D. The corridor felt covered in a fine downy fur.

7. How does the cat's behavior toward Coraline change when they escape?

   A. It was angry that Coraline threw it and ignored her.

   B. It was embarrassed and ran away from Coraline.

   C. It acted friendly toward Coraline by licking her fingers and sitting in her lap.

   D. It acted as if nothing had happened and simply walked away.

Check Your Reading Speed

1분에 몇 단어를 읽는지 리딩 속도를 측정해보세요.

$$\frac{2{,}156 \text{ words}}{\text{reading time ( ) sec}} \times 60 = (\quad) \text{ WPM}$$

Build Your Vocabulary

flat^{복습}
[flæt]

① n. (연립주택, 다세대 주택 등을 포함하는) 아파트식 주거지
② a. 평평한, 균일한; 단호한; n. 평지, 평원
A flat is a set of rooms for living in, usually on one floor and part of a larger building. A flat usually includes a kitchen and bathroom.

transform^{복습}
[trænsfɔ́:rm]

v. 변형하다, 변형시키다; n. 변형
To transform something into something else means to change or convert it into that thing.

depth**
[depθ]

n. 깊이; 깊은 곳, 깊음
The depth of something such as a river or hole is the distance downward from its top surface, or between its upper and lower surfaces.

vermin^{복습}
[və́:rmin]

n. 해충, 기생충; 사회의 해충
Vermin are small animals such as rats and mice which cause problems to humans by carrying disease and damaging crops or food.

stiffen*
[stífən]

v. 굳어지다, 경직되다, 긴장하다
If you stiffen, you stop moving and stand or sit with muscles that are suddenly tense, for example because you feel afraid or angry.

anxious***
[ǽŋkʃəs]

a. 열망하는, 간절히 바라는; 걱정하는, 염려하는
If you are anxious to do something or anxious that something should happen, you very much want to do it or very much want it to happen.

reassure^{복습}
[rì:əʃúər]

vt. 안심시키다 (reassurance n. 안심시키기)
If you reassure someone, you say or do things to make them stop worrying about something.

squeeze^{복습}
[skwi:z]

vt. 꽉 쥐다, 짜다, 압착하다; 쑤셔 넣다; n. 압착, 짜냄
If you squeeze something, you press it firmly, usually with your hands.

suspect*
[səspékt]

v. 의심하다, 혐의를 두다; n. 용의자
If you suspect that something dishonest or unpleasant has been done, you believe that it has probably been done.

frighten^{복습}
[fraitn]

v. 놀라게 하다, 섬뜩하게 하다; 기겁하다 (frightened a. 깜짝 놀란, 겁이 난)
If something or someone frightens you, they cause you to suddenly feel afraid, anxious, or nervous.

liable*
[láiəbl]

a. ~하기 쉬운; 책임을 져야 할, 의무가 있는
When something is liable to happen, it is very likely to happen.

122

bite^{복습}
[bait]

v. 물다, 물어뜯다; n. 물기; 한 입(의 분량)
If an animal or person bites you, they use their teeth to hurt or injure you.

scratch^{복습}
[skrætʃ]

v. 긁다, 할퀴다; n. 할큄, 찰과상
If you scratch yourself, you rub your fingernails against your skin because it is itching.

provoke*
[prəvóuk]

vt. 화나게 하다, 도발하다; 일으키다, 유발시키다
If you provoke someone, you deliberately annoy them and try to make them behave aggressively.

flatly
[flǽtli]

ad. 심드렁하게; 단호히, 딱 잘라서
If you say flatly, you are saying something without expressing any emotion.

hallway^{복습}
[hɔ́:lwèi]

n. 복도; 현관
A hallway in a building is a long passage with doors into rooms on both sides of it.

pretend^{복습}
[priténd]

v. ~인 체하다, 가장하다; a. 가짜의, 꾸민
If you pretend that something is the case, you act in a way that is intended to make people believe that it is the case, although in fact it is not.

brown**
[braun]

v. 갈색이 되(게 하)다; a. 갈색의; (피부가) 갈색인
When food browns it became the color of brown.

core^{복습}
[kɔ:r]

n. (배 · 사과 등의) 응어리, 과심; (사물의) 핵심
The core of a fruit is the central part of it.

plum^{복습}
[plʌm]

n. 자두
A plum is a small, sweet fruit with a smooth red or yellow skin and a stone in the middle.

stone**
[stoun]

n. (복숭아 · 자두등과 같은 과일의) 씨; 돌, 석조
The stone in a plum, cherry, or other fruit is the large hard seed in the middle of it.

formerly*
[fɔ́:rmərli]

ad. 이전에, 예전에
If something happened or was true formerly, it happened or was true in the past.

bunch^{복습}
[bʌntʃ]

n. (과일 등의) 송이, 다발; 다량; 떼, 한패
A bunch of things is a number of things, especially a large number.

rake**
[reik]

v. 긁다 · 문지르다; 긁어 모으다, 샅샅이 캐내다; n. 갈퀴
To rake means to scratch or scrape.

claw^{복습}
[klɔ:]

v. 발톱으로 할퀴다; n. (날카롭고 굽은) 갈고리발톱, 집게발
If an animal claws at something, it scratches or damages it with its claws.

impatient^{복습}
[impéiʃənt]

a. 성급한, 조급한, 참을성 없는
If you are impatient, you are annoyed because you have to wait too long for something.

plain ^{복습}
[plein]

a. 무늬가 없는, 꾸밈없는; 분명한, 명백한; n. 평지, 평야
A plain object, surface, or fabric is entirely in one color and has no pattern, design, or writing on it.

mist ^{복습}
[mist]

n. 안개; v. 안개가 끼다, 눈이 흐려지다
Mist consists of a large number of tiny drops of water in the air, which make it difficult to see very far.

unravel
[ʌnrǽvəl]

v. 풀다, 해명하다, 해결하다
If you unravel a mystery or puzzle, or if it unravels, it gradually becomes clearer and you can work out the answer to it.

mantelpiece ^{복습}
[mǽntlpiːs]

n. 벽난로 위 선반
A mantelpiece is a wood or stone shelf which is the top part of a border round a fireplace.

deceive **
[disíːv]

v. 속이다, 기만하다
If you deceive someone, you make them believe something that is not true, usually in order to get some advantage for yourself.

resemble ^{복습}
[rizémbl]

vt. ~을 닮다, ~와 공통점이 있다 (resemblance n. 닮은 사람; 유사)
If one thing or person resembles another, they are similar to each other.

pale ^{복습}
[peil]

a. 창백한, 엷은, 연한, 희미한; v. 엷어지(게 하)다
If someone looks pale, their face looks a lighter color than usual, usually because they are ill, frightened, or shocked.

belly *
[béli]

n. 배, 복부
The belly of a person or animal is their stomach or abdomen.

writhe ^{복습}
[raið]

v. 몸부림치다, 몸을 뒤틀다; n. 몸부림, 뒹굴기; 고뇌
If you writhe, your body twists and turns violently backward and forward, usually because you are in great pain or discomfort.

twine ^{복습}
[twain]

v. (~을) 휘감(기게 하)다; n. 꼰 실, 꼬기, 감김; 엉클어짐, 뒤얽힘
If you twine one thing around another, or if one thing twines around another, the first thing is twisted or wound around the second.

lean ^{복습}
[liːn]

① v. 상체를 굽히다, 기울다; 의지하다; ~을 기대어 세우다 ② a. 야윈, 마른
If you lean on or against someone or something, you rest against them so that they partly support your weight.

armchair ^{복습}
[áːrmtʃɛər]

n. 안락의자, 팔걸이 의자
An armchair is a big comfortable chair which has a support on each side for your arms.

adjust **
[ədʒʌst]

v. ~을 (장소·위치 등에) 맞추다, 조절하다, 조정하다
If you adjust something such as your clothing or a machine, you correct or alter its position or setting.

frost *
[frɔːst]

v. 서리로 덮다, 서리가 앉다; n. 서리 (frosted a. 반투명의; 서리가 내린)
Frosted glass is glass that you cannot see through clearly.

clink
[kliŋk]

v. 쨍그랑하는 소리를 내다; n. (유리 등의) 땡그랑 소리
If objects clink or if you clink them, they touch each other and make a short, light sound.

124

slip^{복습}
[slip]

v. 슬며시 두다; 살짝 나오다[들어가다]; 미끄러지다
If you slip something somewhere, you put it there quickly in a way that does not attract attention.

intention**
[inténʃən]

n. 의향, 의지, 목적, 의도
An intention is an idea or plan of what you are going to do.

look daggers (at someone)

phrasal v. (분노 · 협박 · 증오의 눈초리로) 노려보다
When you look daggers at someone, you look at them very angrily but not say anything.

cellar^{복습}
[sélər]

n. 지하 저장실
A cellar is a room underneath a building, which is often used for storing things in.

unhook
[ʌnhúk]

v. (갈고리 등에 걸린 것을) 떼어 내다[벗기다]; 걸쇠를 끄르다[벗기다]
If you unhook a piece of clothing that is fastened with hooks, you undo the hooks.

stand to reason

idiom 당연하다, 도리에 맞다
If you say it stands to reason that something is true or likely to happen, you mean that it is obvious.

statue^{복습}
[stǽtʃuː]

n. 상(像), 조각상
A statue is a large sculpture of a person or an animal, made of stone or metal.

passageway^{복습}
[pǽsidʒwèi]

n. 통로, 복도
A passageway is a long narrow space with walls or fences on both sides, which connects one place or room with another.

nod^{복습}
[nɔd]

v. 끄덕이다, 끄덕여 표시하다; n. (동의 · 인사 · 신호 · 명령의) 끄덕임
If you nod, you move your head downward and upward to show agreement, understanding, or approval.

creep^{복습}
[kriːp]

vi. (crept–crept) 천천히[살금살금] 걷다, 기다; n. 포복
If something creeps somewhere, it moves very slowly.

gloat
[glout]

vi. 흡족한 듯이 바라보다
If someone is gloating, they are showing pleasure at their own success or at other people's failure in an arrogant and unpleasant way.

stir^{복습}
[stəːr]

v. 움직이다; 휘젓다; n. 움직임; 휘젓기
If you stir, you move slightly, for example because you are uncomfortable or beginning to wake up.

mechanism*
[mékənizm]

n. 기계(장치), 기구
In a machine or piece of equipment, a mechanism is a part, often consisting of a set of smaller parts, which performs a particular function.

clunk^{복습}
[klʌŋk]

n. 쾅[쿵] (무거운 두 물체가 부딪쳐 나는 둔탁한 소리)
A clunk is a sound made by a heavy object hitting something hard.

reveal^{복습}
[rivíːl]

vt. 드러내다, 보이다, 나타내다
If you reveal something that has been out of sight, you uncover it so that people can see it.

corridor^{복습}
[kɔ́:ridər]

n. 복도
A corridor is a long passage in a building or train, with doors and rooms on one or both sides.

expression^{복습}
[ikspréʃən]

n. 표정, 표현, 표현법
Your expression is the way that your face looks at a particular moment. It shows what you are thinking or feeling.

yowl
[jaul]

vi. 길고 슬프게 짖다, 신음하다; n. 구슬프게 짖는 소리
If a person or an animal yowls, they make a long loud cry, especially because they are sad or in pain.

flail
[fleil]

v. 휘두르다; 도리깨질하다; n. 도리깨
If your arms or legs flail or if you flail them about, they wave about in an energetic but uncontrolled way.

bare^{복습}
[bɛər]

v. 드러내다; a. 벌거벗은; 있는 그대로의; 텅 빈
If you bare something, you uncover it and show it.

fierce*
[fiərs]

a. 사나운; 격렬한, 지독한
A fierce animal or person is very aggressive or angry.

ululate
[ʌ́ljulèit]

v. (길게 소리 내어) 울다, 울부짖다
If someone ululates, they make quickly repeated loud sounds, often to express sorrow or happiness.

sink^{복습}
[siŋk]

v. (sank-sunk) 밀어넣다, 가라앉히다; 가라앉다, 빠지다; n. (부엌의) 싱크대, 개수대
If something sharp sinks or is sunk into something solid, it goes deeply into it.

stuff^{복습}
[stʌf]

n. 물질, 물건; vt. 채워 넣다, 속을 채우다
You can use stuff to refer to things such as a substance, a collection of things, events, or ideas, or the contents of something in a general way without mentioning the thing itself by name.

hiss^{복습}
[his]

v. 쉿 하는 소리를 내다; n. 쉿 (제지·힐책의 소리)
To hiss means to make a sound like a long 's'.

swipe
[swaip]

v. 힘껏 치다; 훔치다; 벌떡벌떡 들이켜다; n. 강타, 맹타; 비난
If you swipe at a person or thing, you try to hit them with a stick or other object, making a swinging movement with your arm.

scalpel
[skǽlpəl]

n. (수술용) 메스
A scalpel is a knife with a short, thin, sharp blade. Scalpels are used by surgeons during operations.

ooze
[u:z]

n. 분비물; 스며나옴; v. 스며나오다, 새어나오다
Ooze is the liquid which flows slowly and in small quantities.

trickle^{복습}
[trikl]

vi. 똑똑 떨어지다, 졸졸 흐르다; n. 물방울, 실개울
If liquid trickles somewhere, it flows slowly and without force in a thin line.

gash
[gæʃ]

n. 깊은 상처; (지면의) 갈라진 틈; vt. 상처를 입히다
A gash is a long, deep cut in your skin or in the surface of something.

126

spring***
[spriŋ]

v. (sprang–sprung) 튀다, 뛰어오르다; n. 뜀, 뛰어오름; 샘, 수원지; (계절) 봄
When a person or animal springs, they jump upward or forward suddenly or quickly.

hesitate복습
[hézətèit]

v. 주저하다, 머뭇거리다, 망설이다
If you hesitate, you do not speak or act for a short time, usually because you are uncertain, embarrassed, or worried about what you are going to say or do.

phantom
[fǽntəm]

a. 환영의, 유령의; n. 환영, 허깨비, 환상
You use phantom to describe something which you think you experience but which is not real.

aware복습
[əwéər]

a. 알고 있는, 의식하고 있는, 알아차린
If you are aware of something, you realize that it is present or is happening because you hear it, see it, smell it, or feel it.

somehow복습
[sʌ́mhàu]

ad. 여하튼, 어쨌든; 어쩐지, 아무래도
You use somehow to say that you do not know or cannot say how something was done or will be done.

insubstantial
[insəbstǽnʃəl]

a. 실체가 없는; 대단찮은, 견고하지 않은
Something that is insubstantial is not large, solid, or strong.

let up

phrasal v. 그만두다, (강도가) 약해지다
If you let up something, you do it with less effort or energy than before, or stop doing it.

whisper복습
[hwíspəːr]

v. 속삭이다
When you whisper, you say something very quietly.

madden
[mǽdn]

v. ~를 미치게[정말 화나게] 만들다
To madden a person or animal means to make them very angry.

infuriate
[infjúərièit]

vt. 격노하게 하다, 격분시키다
If something or someone infuriates you, they make you extremely angry.

glorious*
[glɔ́ːriəs]

a. 아름다운, 훌륭한; 영광스러운, 찬란한
Something that is glorious is very beautiful and impressive.

faint복습
[feint]

a. 희미한, 어렴풋한; vi. 기절하다 (faintly ad. 희미하게, 어렴풋이)
A faint sound, color, mark, feeling, or quality has very little strength or intensity.

snatch복습
[snætʃ]

v. 와락 붙잡다, 잡아채다; n. 잡아 뺏음, 강탈
If you snatch something or snatch at something, you take it or pull it away quickly.

jerk복습
[dʒəːrk]

v. 갑자기 움직이다; n. (갑자기) 홱 움직임; 반사 운동
If you jerk something or someone in a particular direction, or they jerk in a particular direction, they move a short distance very suddenly and quickly.

duck복습
[dʌk]

① v. 피하다, 머리를 홱 숙이다 ② n. 오리
If you duck, you move your head or the top half of your body quickly downward to avoid something that might hit you, or to avoid being seen.

possess ^{복습}
[pəzés]

vt. 소유하다, 가지고 있다
If you possess something, you have it or own it.

resist ^{복습}
[rizíst]

v. 저항하다, 반대하다, 방해하다 (resistance n. 저항, 반항)
If you resist doing something, or resist the temptation to do it, you stop yourself from doing it although you would like to do it.

crash ^{복습}
[kræʃ]

n. 쿵, 와르르 하는 소리; 충돌, 추락; vt. 충돌하다, 추락하다
A crash is a sudden, loud noise.

bang ^{복습}
[bæŋ]

v. 탕 치다, 부딪치다, 쾅 닫(히)다; n. 쾅 하는 소리
If you bang a door or if it bangs, it closes suddenly with a loud noise.

height ^{복습}
[hait]

n. 높이; (사람의) 키, 신장
Height is the quality of being tall.

sort ^{복습}
[sɔːrt]

n. 종류, 부류; vt. 분류하다, 골라내다
If you talk about a particular sort of something, you are talking about a class of things that have particular features in common.

scuttle ^{복습}
[skʌtl]

vi. 급히 가다, 황급히 달리다; 허둥지둥 도망가다
When people or small animals scuttle somewhere, they run there with short quick steps.

thump ^{복습}
[θʌmp]

n. 탁[쿵] 하는 소리; 때림, 세게 쥐어박음; v. 부딪치다
A thump is a loud, dull sound by hitting something.

bump ^{복습}
[bʌmp]

v. (쾅 하고) 부딪치다, 충돌하다; n. 충돌, 혹
If you bump into something or someone, you accidentally hit them while you are moving.

uphill
[ʌphil]

a. 힘드는, 애먹는; 올라가는, 오르막의; ad. 언덕 위로; 고생하여
If you refer to something as an uphill struggle or an uphill battle, you mean that it requires a great deal of effort and determination, but it should be possible to achieve it.

yielding
[jíːldiŋ]

a. 유연한, 잘 구부러지는; 양보를 잘 하는
A yielding surface or object is quite soft and will move or bend rather than staying stiff if you put pressure on it.

downy
[dáuni]

a. 솜털 같은, 부드러운
Something that is downy is filled or covered with small soft feathers.

howl ^{복습}
[haul]

v. (바람 등이) 윙윙거리다; 짖다, 울부짖다; n. 울부짖는 소리
When the wind howls, it blows hard and makes a loud noise.

wail ^{복습}
[weil]

n. 울부짖음, 한탄; v. (큰소리로) 투덜거리다, 울부짖다
If you wail something, you say it in a loud, high-pitched voice that shows that you are unhappy or in pain.

glow ^{복습}
[ɡlou]

v. 빛을 내다; n. 빛, 밝음
If something glows, it produces a dull, steady light.

patch ^{복습}
[pætʃ]

n. 부분, 단편, 파편; 헝겊 조각; 반창고; v. 헝겊을 대고 깁다
A patch on a surface is a part of it which is different in appearance from the area around it.

128

pad^{복습}
[pæd]

① v. 거닐다, 발소리를 내지 않고 걷다; ② vt. ~에 덧대다; n. 덧대는 것. 패드
When someone pads somewhere, they walk there with steps that are fairly quick, light, and quiet.

momentum
[mouméntəm]

n. 기세 · 여세
If a process or movement gains momentum, it keeps developing or happening more quickly and keeps becoming less likely to stop.

daylight^{복습}
[déilàit]

n. 일광, 빛; 낮
Daylight is the natural light that there is during the day, before it gets dark.

puff^{복습}
[pʌf]

v. 숨을 헐떡이다, (연기를) 내뿜다; 부풀어 오르다; n. 훅 불기, 숨, 입김
If you are puffing, you are breathing loudly and quickly with your mouth open because you are out of breath after a lot of physical effort.

wheeze
[hwi:z]

v. 씨근거리다, 숨을 헐떡이며 말하다; n. 씨근거리는 소리, 숨을 헐떡이는 소리
If someone wheezes, they breathe with difficulty and make a whistling sound.

wraith
[reiθ]

n. 망령, 유령
A wraith is a ghost.

pant^{복습}
[pænt]

vi. 헐떡거리다, 숨차다; n. 헐떡거림, 숨 가쁨
If you pant, you breathe quickly and loudly with your mouth open, because you have been doing something energetic.

stagger[*]
[stǽgər]

v. 비틀거리다, 휘청거리다; n. 비틀거림
If you stagger, you walk very unsteadily, for example because you are ill or drunk.

slam[*]
[slæm]

v. (문 따위를) 탕 닫다, 세게 치다; 털썩 내려놓다; n. 쾅 (하는 소리)
If you slam a door or window or if it slams, it shuts noisily and with great force.

huddle[*]
[hʌdl]

v. 움츠리다, 둥글게 말다, (떼 지어) 몰리다; n. 군중, 무리
If you huddle somewhere, you sit, stand, or lie there holding your arms and legs close to your body, usually because you are cold or frightened.

farthest^{복습}
[fɑ́:rðist]

a. (far–farther–farthest) 가장 먼; ad. 가장 멀리(에)
Something farthest is at the greatest distance in space, direction or time.

tip^{복습}
[tip]

① n. (뾰족한) 끝 ② v. 기울이다; 뒤집(히)다 ③ n. 팁, 사례금
The tip of something long and narrow is the end of it.

crouch^{복습}
[krautʃ]

v. 몸을 쭈그리다, 쪼그리고 앉다; 웅크리다; n. 웅크림
If you are crouching, your legs are bent under you so that you are close to the ground and leaning forward slightly.

distract^{복습}
[distrǽkt]

vt. (마음 · 주의를) 흐트러뜨리다, 딴 데로 돌리다
If something distracts you or your attention from something, it takes your attention away from it.

sandpaper
[sǽndpèipər]

n. 사포, 샌드페이퍼; v. 사포로 닦다 (sandpapery a. 까칠까칠한, 거친)
Sandpaper is strong paper that has a coating of sand on it. It is used for rubbing wood or metal surfaces to make them smoother.

purr
[pəːr]

v. (기분 좋은 듯이) 그르렁거리다, 부르릉 하는 소리를 내다; n. 그르렁거리는 소리
When a cat purrs, it makes a low vibrating sound with its throat because it is contented.

lap복습
[læp]

n. 무릎; 한 바퀴; v. 겹치게 하다
If you have something on your lap, it is on top of your legs and near to your body.

fade복습
[feid]

vi. 희미해지다, 바래다, 시들다
When a colored object fades or when the light fades it, it gradually becomes paler.

horizon복습
[həráizn]

n. 지평선, 수평선
The horizon is the line in the far distance where the sky seems to meet the land or the sea.

crack복습
[kræk]

v. 금이 가다; 깨다, 부수다; n. 조금, 약간; 갈라진 금; 갑작스런 날카로운 소리
(cracked a. 깨진, 금이 간)
If something hard cracks, or if you crack it, it becomes slightly damaged, with lines appearing on its surface.

bark복습
[bɑːrk]

① n. 나무 껍질 ② v. 짖다; 고함치다, 소리 지르며 말하다
Bark is the tough material that covers the outside of a tree.

whisker복습
[wískəːr]

n. (고양이 · 쥐 등의) 수염; 구레나룻
The whiskers of an animal such as a cat or a mouse are the long stiff hairs that grow near its mouth.

barely복습
[béərli]

ad. 거의 ~않다; 간신히, 가까스로
You use barely to say that something is only just true or only just the case.

wriggle복습
[rigl]

v. 꿈틀거리다, 몸부림치다; n. 몸부림침, 꿈틀거림
If you wriggle or wriggle part of your body, you twist and turn with quick movements.

curl복습
[kəːrl]

vt. 꼬다, 곱슬곱슬하게 하다; n. 컬, 곱슬머리
If your toes, fingers, or other parts of your body curl, or if you curl them, they form a curved or round shape.

130

chapter twelve

1. Which of the following was NOT one of the items
   Coraline found in the pockets of her dressing gown?
   A. A black key
   B. A button eye
   C. A stone with a hole in it
   D. An empty snow globe

2. What did Coraline do with the black key?
   A. She broke it in half so that it could never be used again.
   B. She strung the key on a string and wore it around her neck.
   C. She put it back in the kitchen where it belonged.
   D. She put it back in the pocket of her dressing gown.

3. How did Coraline's father react to Coraline?
   A. He ignored her and told her to go away.
   B. He told her to go help her mother with dinner in the kitchen.
   C. He picked her up and carried her into the kitchen.
   D. He wondered how she had defeated the other mother by herself.

4. After Coraline put the marbles under her pillow and fell asleep, what kind of dream did she have about the three other children?
   A. She dreamed they all had a picnic outdoors and played together.
   B. She dreamed that they had to go back to fight the other mother again.
   C. She dreamed that they went to a far away planet and watched the stars.
   D. She dreamed that they all ate delicious food together at a restaurant.

5. How did Coraline realize that it was a dream when they were playing games?
   A. They could all turn into ghosts.
   B. They could all fly around.
   C. They didn't get sick from all the food they had eaten.
   D. They never got tired or winded when playing.

6. What did the children tell Coraline before they left?
   A. They told her that the other mother would forget about her.
   B. They told her to make sure that the door was actually locked.
   C. They told her that things were still not over for her.
   D. They told her to stop worrying and just enjoy life.

7. What did Coraline find strange about the scuttling sound down the hall?
   A. It sounded as if it had odd and irregular footsteps.
   B. It sounded as if it were coming from inside the walls.
   C. It sounded as if it might have been a bird.
   D. It sounded as if it was the cat she had met.

1분에 몇 단어를 읽는지 리딩 속도를 측정해보세요.

$$\frac{1{,}975 \text{ words}}{\text{reading time (} \quad \text{) sec}} \times 60 = (\quad) \text{ WPM}$$

Build Your Vocabulary

bullet**
[búlit]

n. (소총 · 권총의) 총탄, 탄환
A bullet is a small piece of metal with a pointed or rounded end, which is fired out of a gun.

trip***
[trip]

v. 걸려 넘어지다; 경쾌한 걸음걸이로 걷다; n. 여행
If you trip when you are walking, you knock your foot against something and fall or nearly fall.

ointment
[ɔ́intmənt]

n. 연고, 고약(膏藥)
An ointment is a smooth thick substance that is put on sore skin or a wound to help it heal.

scrape*복습
[skreip]

n. 긁힌 상처, 찰과상; 긁기; v. 긁(어내)다, 벗겨내다, 떼다
A scrape is a part damaged or cleaned by scraping.

marble*복습
[ma.rbl]

n. 구슬, 구슬치기; 대리석
A marble is one of the small balls used in the game of marbles.

glitter*복습
[glítər]

vi. 반짝반짝 빛나다, 반짝이다; n. 반짝거림, 광채
(glittery a. 반짝반짝 빛나는, 눈이 부신)
If something glitters, light comes from or is reflected off different parts of it.

swirl*복습
[swə:rl]

vi. 소용돌이치다, 빙빙 돌다
If liquid or flowing swirls, it moves round and round quickly.

string*복습
[striŋ]

n. 끈, 줄, 실; v. (strung–strung) 묶다, 매달다, 꿰다
String is thin rope made of twisted threads, used for tying things together or tying up parcels.

knot**
[nat]

v. 얽히게 하다, 매다; n. 매듭; 나무 마디
If you knot a piece of string, rope, cloth, or other material, you pass one end or part of it through a loop and pull it tight.

hallway*복습
[hɔ́:lwèi]

n. 복도; 현관
A hallway in a building is a long passage with doors into rooms on both sides of it.

creep*복습
[kri:p]

vi. (crept–crept) 천천히[살금살금] 걷다, 기다; n. 포복
If something creeps somewhere, it moves very slowly.

bald*
[bɔ:ld]

vi. 머리가 벗겨지다; a. (머리 등이) 벗어진, 대머리의
(balding a. 머리가 벗겨지기 시작한)
Someone who is balding is beginning to lose the hair on the top of their head.

134

crust ^{복습}
[krʌst]

n. (빵) 껍질; 딱딱한 층, 표면
The crust on a loaf of bread is the outside part.

alternate*
[ɔ́:ltərnèit]

v. 번갈아 하다, 교대시키다 (alternately ad. 번갈아, 교대로)
When you alternate two things, you keep using one then the other.

dough ^{복습}
[dou]

n. 반죽 덩어리; 굽지 않는 빵, 가루 반죽 (doughy a. 밀가루 반죽같은)
Dough is a fairly firm mixture of flour, water, and sometimes also fat and sugar.

chunk*
[tʃʌŋk]

n. 큰 덩어리, 상당한 양[액수]; v. 덩어리로 나누다
A chunk of something is a large amount or large part of it.

entire ^{복습}
[intáiər]

a. 전체의; 완전한
You use entire when you want to emphasize that you are referring to the whole of something, for example, the whole of a place, time, or population.

meadow ^{복습}
[médou]

n. 목초지, 초원
A meadow is a field which has grass and flowers growing in it.

fluffy ^{복습}
[flʌfi]

a. 푹신한, 보풀의, 솜털의
If you describe something such as a towel or a toy animal as fluffy, you mean that it is very soft.

horizon ^{복습}
[həráizn]

n. 지평선, 수평선
The horizon is the line in the far distance where the sky seems to meet the land or the sea.

untroubled
[ʌntrʌ́bld]

a. 흐트러짐이 없는, 고요한; 마음이 산란하지 않은
If you are untroubled by something, you are not affected or worried by it.

jug*
[dʒʌg]

n. 물주전자, 단지
A jug is a container with a handle and is used for holding and pouring liquids.

tablecloth*
[téiblklɔ̀:θ]

n. 식탁[테이블]보
A tablecloth is a cloth used to cover a table.

odd ^{복습}
[ɑd]

a. 이상한, 기묘한
If you describe someone or something as odd, you think that they are strange or unusual.

frill
[fril]

n. 가장자리 주름 장식; 뽐냄, 우쭐거림, 허식 (frilly a. 주름장식이 많은)
A frill is a long narrow strip of cloth or paper with many folds in it, which is attached to something as a decoration.

wonder ^{복습}
[wʌ́ndər]

v. 호기심을 가지다, 이상하게 여기다; n. 경탄할 만한 것, 경이
If you wonder about something, you think about it, either because it interests you and you want to know more about it, or because you are worried or suspicious about it.

opposite
[ɑ́pəzit]

prep. 건너편[맞은편]에; a. 다른 쪽의, 건너편의; (정)반대의
If one thing is opposite another, it is on the other side of a space from it.

chapter twelve

grateful**
[gréitfəl]

a. 고맙게 여기는, 감사하는
If you are grateful for something that someone has given you or done for you, you have warm, friendly feelings toward them and wish to thank them.

deft
[deft]

a. 손재주 있는, 솜씨 좋은 (deftly **ad.** 솜씨 좋게, 교묘히)
A deft action is skillful and often quick.

loaf^{복습}
[louf]

n. (모양을 만들어 한 덩어리로 구운) 빵 한 덩이
A loaf of bread is bread which has been shaped and baked in one piece.

pale^{복습}
[peil]

a. 창백한; 엷은, 연한, 희미한; **v.** 엷어지(게 하)다
If someone looks pale, their face looks a lighter color than usual, usually because they are ill, frightened, or shocked.

swear^{복습}
[swɛər]

v. (swore−sworn) 단언하다, 맹세하다; 욕을 하다; **n.** 맹세, 선서
If you swear to do something, you promise in a serious way that you will do it.

immense*
[iméns]

a. 막대한, 무한한, 광대한 (immensely **ad.** 아주, 굉장히)
If you describe something as immense, you mean that it is extremely large or great.

toss^{복습}
[tɔːs]

v. 던지다, 내던지다
If you toss something somewhere, you throw it there lightly, often in a rather careless way.

winded
[wíndid]

a. 숨이 찬
If you are winded by something such as a blow, the air is suddenly knocked out of your lungs so that you have difficulty breathing for a short time.

sweat*
[swet]

v. 땀 흘리다; 습기가 차다; **n.** 땀
When you sweat, drops of liquid comes through your skin.

magnificent*
[mægnífəsnt]

a. 멋진, 근사한; 웅장한, 장엄한
If you say that something or someone is magnificent, you mean that you think they are extremely good, beautiful, or impressive.

romp
[rɑmp]

n. 떠들며 뛰어놀기, 활발한 장난; **v.** 떠들썩하게 뛰놀다
When children or animals romp, they play noisily and happily.

flutter^{복습}
[flʌtəːr]

v. (새 등이) 날갯짓하다, (깃발 등이) 펄럭이다; **n.** 펄럭임
If something light such as a small bird or a piece of paper flutters somewhere, it moves through the air with small quick movements.

swoop^{복습}
[swuːp]

v. 급강하하다, 내리 덮치다
When a bird or airplane swoops, it suddenly moves downward through the air in a smooth curving movement.

grab^{복습}
[græb]

v. 부여잡다, 움켜쥐다; **n.** 부여잡기
If you grab something, you take it or pick it up suddenly and roughly.

swing^{복습}
[swiŋ]

v. 빙 돌다, 휙 돌리다, 회전시키다; 휘두르다, 흔들다; 매달리다
If something swings in a particular direction or if you swing it in that direction, it moves in that direction with a smooth, curving movement.

136

relish^{복습}
[réliʃ]

n. 즐거움, 흥미, 의욕; 맛, 풍미; v. 즐기다; 기쁘게 생각하다
If you do something with relish, you feel pleasant.

nibble
[nibl]

v. 조금씩 물어뜯다, 갉아먹다; n. 조금씩 물어뜯기, 한 입 분량
If you nibble food, you eat it by biting very small pieces of it.

blossom^{**}
[blásəm]

n. 꽃; vi. 꽃 피다, 개화하다
Blossom is the flowers that appear on a tree before the fruit.

reward^{**}
[riwɔ́:rd]

v. 보답하다, 보상하다; n. 현상금, 보상금; 보상, 보답
If you do something and are rewarded with a particular benefit, you receive that benefit as a result of doing that thing.

smear
[smiər]

n. 얼룩; 비방; v. 더럽히다; (기름 등을) 바르다, 칠하다; (잉크 등이) 번지다
A smear is a dirty or oily mark.

circlet
[sɔ́:rklit]

n. (꽃이나 귀금속 등으로 만든 머리에 쓰는) 관
A circlet is a small circle or ring, especially a circular ornament worn on the head.

set out

phrasa v. (여행 등을) 떠나다, 출발하다; 착수하다, 시도하다
When you set out to somewhere, you leave a place and begin a journey, especially a long journey.

uncharted
[ʌnʧá:rt]

a. 미지의, 잘 알지 못하는; 지도에 표시되어 있지 않은
If you describe a situation, experience, or activity as uncharted territory or waters, you mean that it is new or unfamiliar.

tremble^{복습}
[trembl]

v. 떨다, 떨리다
If you tremble, you shake slightly because you are frightened or cold.

shift[*]
[ʃift]

v. 방향을 바꾸다, 옮기다; n. 변화, 이동; 교대
If you shift something or if it shifts, it moves slightly.

squeeze^{복습}
[skwi:z]

vt. 꽉 쥐다, 짜다, 압착하다; 쑤셔 넣다; n. 압착, 짜냄
If you squeeze something, you press it firmly, usually with your hands.

reassure^{복습}
[ri:əʃúər]

vt. 안심시키다
If you reassure someone, you say or do things to make them stop worrying about something.

clue^{복습}
[klu:]

n. 단서, 실마리
A clue is a sign or some information which helps you to find the answer to a problem.

governess^{복습}
[gʌvərnis]

n. (아이들의 예절 · 교육을 맡는) 여자 가정교사
A governess is a woman who is employed by a family to live with them and educate their children.

shrug^{복습}
[ʃrʌg]

v. (양 손바닥을 내보이면서 어깨를) 으쓱하다; n. 으쓱하기
If you shrug, you raise your shoulders to show that you are not interested in something or that you do not know or care about something.

wisdom^{복습}
[wízdəm]

n. 지혜, 현명함
Wisdom is the ability to use your experience and knowledge in order to make sensible decisions or judgments.

bless*
[bles]

vt. 축복하다, 은총을 내리다 (blessing n. 축복, 하늘의 은총)
When someone such as a priest blesses people or things, he asks for God's favor and protection for them.

abundance*
[əbÁndəns]

n. 풍부, 많음; 부유
An abundance of something is a large quantity of it.

blurt
[blə:rt]

vt. 불쑥 말하다; 무심결에 누설하다
If someone blurts something, they say it suddenly, after trying hard to keep quiet or to keep it secret.

tricky
[tríki]

a. 교묘한, 까다로운
If you describe a task or problem as tricky, you mean that it is difficult to do or deal with.

whisper복습
[hwíspə:r]

v. 속삭이다
When you whisper, you say something very quietly.

twinkle복습
[twíŋkl]

v. 반짝반짝 빛나다; 깜빡이다; n. 반짝거림
If a star or a light twinkles, it shines with an unsteady light which rapidly and constantly changes from bright to faint.

wave복습
[weiv]

v. 흔들다; 물결치다; n. 흔들기; 물결, 파도
If you wave or wave your hand, you move your hand from side to side in the air, usually in order to say hello or goodbye to someone.

convince*
[kənvíns]

vt. 설득하다, 확신시키다, 납득시키다 (convinced a. 확신하는)
If someone or something convinces you of something, they make you believe that it is true or that it exists.

rustle복습
[rʌsl]

vi. 바스락거리다, 살랑살랑 소리 내다; n. 바스락거리는 소리
(rustling a. 와삭와삭[바스락바스락] 소리 나는, 옷 스치는 소리가 나는)
If things such as paper or leaves rustle, or if you rustle them, they move about and make a soft, dry sound.

rattle복습
[rætl]

v. 왈각달각 소리 나다, 덜걱덜걱 움직이다; n. 덜거덕거리는 소리
When something rattles or when you rattle it, it makes short sharp knocking sounds because it is being shaken or it keeps hitting against something hard.

clamber복습
[klǽmbər]

vi. 기어 올라가다
If you clamber somewhere, you climb there with difficulty, usually using your hands as well as your feet.

pause복습
[pɔ:z]

n. 멈춤, 중지; vi. 잠시 멈추다, 중단하다
A pause is a short period when you stop doing something before continuing.

scuttle복습
[skʌtl]

vi. 급히 가다, 황급히 달리다; 허둥지둥 도망가다
When people or small animals scuttle somewhere, they run there with short quick steps.

predawn
[pri:dɔ́:n]

a., n. 동트기 전(의)
If you do something in predawn, you do it before the rising of the sun.

138

corridor[복습]
[kɔ́:ridər]

n. 복도
A corridor is a long passage in a building or train, with doors and rooms on one or both sides.

desert[복습]
[dizə́:rt]

① v. 버리다, 유기하다; 인적이 끊기다 (deserted a. 황량한, 사람이 살지 않는)
② n. 사막, 황무지
If people or animals desert a place, they leave it and it becomes empty.

spare[복습]
[spεər]

v. 할애하다; 아끼다, 절약하다; a. 예비의, 여분의; n. 예비품, 비상용품
If you spare time or another resource for a particular purpose, you make it available for that purpose.

hasty*
[héisti]

a. 급한, 성급한
A hasty movement, action, or statement is sudden, and often done in reaction to something that has just happened.

glance[복습]
[glæns]

n. 흘긋 봄; v. 흘긋 보다, 잠깐 보다
A glance is a quick look at someone or something.

wardrobe[복습]
[wɔ́:rdròub]

n. 옷장; 의상
A wardrobe is a tall cupboard or cabinet in which you can hang your clothes.

snore[복습]
[snɔ́:r]

n. 코 고는 소리; v. 코를 골다
Snore is a snorting or grunting sound in a person's breathing while asleep.

couch*
[kautʃ]

n. 소파, 긴 의자
A couch is a long, comfortable seat for two or three people.

detach*
[ditǽtʃ]

v. 분리하다, 떼어놓다
If one thing detaches from another, it becomes separated from it.

scrabble[복습]
[skrǽbl]

v. 헤적여 찾다, 긁어모으다; 휘갈겨 쓰다, 낙서하다; n. 휘갈겨 쓰기, 낙서
If you scrabble for something, especially something that you cannot see, you move your hands or your feet about quickly and hurriedly in order to find it.

rush[복습]
[rʌʃ]

n. 돌진, 급습; 혼잡, 쇄도; v. 서두르다, 돌진하다
A rush is a situation in which you need to go somewhere or do something very quickly.

click[복습]
[klik]

v. 찰칵[딸깍]하는 소리를 내다; n. 찰칵[딸깍](하는 소리)
If something clicks or if you click it, it makes a short, sharp sound.

crab*
[kræb]

n. 게 (crablike a. 게 같은)
A crab is a sea creature with a flat round body covered by a shell, and five pairs of legs with large claws on the front pair.

tap[복습]
[tæp]

① v. 가볍게 두드리다; n. 가볍게 두드리기 ② n. 주둥이, (수도 등의) 꼭지
If you tap something, you hit it with a quick light blow or a series of quick light blows.

scurry[복습]
[skə́:ri]

vi. 종종걸음으로 달리다, 급히 가다
When people or small animals scurry somewhere, they move there quickly and hurriedly, especially because they are frightened.

clutch^{복습}
[klʌtʃ]

v. 꽉 잡다, 붙들다, 부여잡다; n. 움켜쥠; 지배(력), 수중
If you clutch at something or clutch something, you hold it tightly, usually because you are afraid or anxious.

snatch^{복습}
[snætʃ]

v. 와락 붙잡다, 잡아채다; n. 잡아 뺏음, 강탈
If you snatch something or snatch at something, you take it or pull it away quickly.

pop^{복습}
[pap]

v. (물건을) 쏙 넣다; 뻥 하고 터지다; 불쑥 움직이다; n. 뻥[탁] 하는 소리; 발포
If you pop something somewhere, you put it there quickly.

obedient[*]
[oubí:diənt]

a. 순종하는, 고분고분한 (obediently ad. 고분고분하게)
A person or animal who is obedient does what they are told to do.

crimson^{복습}
[krímzən]

a. 진홍색의; n. 진홍색
Something that is crimson is deep red in color.

chapter thirteen

1. How did Coraline's parents feel about their time in the snow globe?
   A. They were frightened by what had happened.
   B. They didn't seem to remember what happened.
   C. They thought it had been exciting.
   D. They were very worried about Coraline.

2. What happened to the marbles under Coraline's pillow?
   A. They had all disappeared completely.
   B. They had been taken by the other mother.
   C. They had become broken and empty of whatever was inside.
   D. They rolled off and were on the floor.

3. Why did Miss Spink need to take Hamish the dog to the vet?
   A. It had gotten sick from some food.
   B. It was time for its annual check-up.
   C. It had grown frightened and wouldn't eat.
   D. It had been injured with a deep gash.

4. What did Coraline do the night the hand was scratching at her bedroom window?

  A. She slept uneasily, sometimes waking up to work on a plan.

  B. She didn't sleep at all and stayed up worrying all night long.

  C. She closed the curtains and made sure the window was locked.

  D. She left her room to try to stop the hand.

5. How did Coraline trick the hand into falling into her trap?

  A. She had a picnic with her dolls to get its attention and then pushed the hand down the well.

  B. She threw the key down the well so that the hand would have to chase it.

  C. She spread a tablecloth over the well so that it fell when it grabbed the key in the center.

  D. She caught the hand in the tablecloth and had the cat help her kill it.

6. According to Mr. Bobo, what did the mice say about Coraline?

  A. They said that Coraline would make a great performer for their circus show.

  B. They said that Coraline was their savior.

  C. They said that Coraline still had work to do in order to keep them safe.

  D. They said Coraline might find another door later.

7. How did Coraline feel the night before the first day of school?

  A. She felt nervous for the new school year, because she wasn't good at schoolwork.

  B. She felt excited, because she really enjoyed schoolwork.

  C. She felt confident, because nothing about school could scare her anymore.

  D. She felt restless, because she still had nightmares about the other mother.

1분에 몇 단어를 읽는지 리딩 속도를 측정해보세요.

$$\frac{2,847 \text{ words}}{\text{reading time ( ) sec}} \times 60 = (\quad) \text{ WPM}$$

Build Your Vocabulary

wonder복습
[wʌ́ndər]
v. 호기심을 가지다, 이상하게 여기다; n. 경탄할 만한 것, 경이
If you wonder about something, you think about it, either because it interests you and you want to know more about it, or because you are worried or suspicious about it.

eventual
[ivénʧuəl]
a. 최후의, 궁극적인
You use eventual to indicate that something happens or is the case at the end of a process or period of time.

conclusion*
[kənklú:ʒən]
n. 결론, 결말
The conclusion of something is its ending.

keep track of
idiom ~에 대해 계속 알고[파악하고] 있다
If you keep track of something, you remember about the number of something or the time.

solid복습
[sálid]
a. 단단한; 견실한, 견고한; n. 고체 (solidly ad. 단결하여, 만장일치로)
A solid substance or object stays the same shape whether it is in a container or not.

marble복습
[ma:rbl]
n. 구슬, 구슬치기; 대리석
A marble is one of the small balls used in the game of marbles.

scrunch
[skrʌnʧ]
vt. 뽀드득 뽀드득 소리를 내다; (머리를) 헝클어뜨리다; n. 우두둑 부서지는 소리
If you scrunch something, you squeeze it or bend it so that it is no longer in its natural shape and is often crushed.

fragment복습
[frǽgmənt]
n. 부서진 조각, 파편, 떨어져 나간 조각
A fragment of something is a small piece or part of it.

shell복습
[ʃel]
n. 껍데기; 조가비; v. 껍데기를 벗기다 (eggshell n. 달걀 껍질)
The shell of a nut or egg is the hard covering which surrounds it.

delicate**
[délikət]
a. 깨지기 쉬운, 약한; 섬세한, 고운; 예민한, 민감한
If something is delicate, it is easy to harm, damage, or break, and needs to be handled or treated carefully.

sphere*
[sfiər]
n. 구, 구체; 영역
A sphere is an object that is completely round in shape like a ball.

gather복습
[gǽðər]
v. 모으다, 모이다
If you gather things, you collect them together so that you can use them.

144

bracelet^{복습}
[bréislit]

n. 팔찌
A bracelet is a chain or band, usually made of metal, which you wear around your wrist as jewelry.

niece^{복습}
[ni:s]

n. 조카딸
Someone's niece is the daughter of their sister or brother.

flat^{복습}
[flæt]

① n. (연립주택, 다세대 주택 등을 포함하는) 아파트식 주거지
② a. 평평한, 균일한; 단호한; n. 평지, 평원
A flat is a set of rooms for living in, usually on one floor and part of a larger building. A flat usually includes a kitchen and bathroom.

insist^{**}
[insíst]

v. 우기다, 주장하다; 강요하다
If you insist that something is the case, you say so very firmly and refuse to say otherwise, even though other people do not believe you.

come up roses

idiom 썩 잘 되어가다
If things come up roses, they produce a positive result, especially when things seemed to be going badly at first.

clump^{복습}
[klʌmp]

n. 수풀, (관목의) 덤불
A clump of things such as trees or plants is a small group of them growing together.

stick^{복습}
[stik]

① v. 달라붙다, 붙이다; 찔러 넣다, 찌르다; 꽂히다, 박히다 ② n. 막대기, 지팡이
If one thing sticks to another, it becomes attached to it and is difficult to remove.

tut
[tʌt]

vi. 혀를 차다; n. 쯧(하고 혀 차기)
If you tut, you make a sound with your tongue touching the top of your mouth when you want to indicate disapproval, annoyance, or sympathy.

spectacle[*]
[spéktəkl]

n. (pl.) 안경; 광경, 장관
Glasses are sometimes referred to as spectacles.

signify[*]
[sígnəfài]

vt. 의미하다, 뜻하다, 알리다
If an event, a sign, or a symbol signifies something, it is a sign of that thing or represents that thing.

sort^{복습}
[sɔ:rt]

n. 종류, 부류; vt. 분류하다, 골라내다
If you talk about a particular sort of something, you are talking about a class of things that have particular features in common.

gash^{복습}
[gæʃ]

n. 깊은 상처; (지면의) 갈라진 틈; vt. 상처를 입히다
A gash is a long, deep cut in your skin or in the surface of something.

vet
[vet]

n. (= veterinarian) 수의사; v. 동물을 진료하다
A vet is someone who is qualified to treat sick or injured animals.

magnificent^{복습}
[mægnífəsnt]

a. 멋진, 근사한; 웅장한, 장엄한
If you say that something or someone is magnificent, you mean that you think they are extremely good, beautiful, or impressive.

make up for something

idiom ~에 대해 보상하다, 만회하다
If you make up for something bad, you do or provide good thing to balance or reduce the effects of it.

miserable복습
[mízərəbl]

a. 지독한, 불쌍한, 비참한
If you describe a place or situation as miserable, you mean that it makes you feel unhappy or depressed.

glorious복습
[glɔ́:riəs]

a. 아름다운, 훌륭한; 영광스러운, 찬란한
Something that is glorious is very beautiful and impressive.

railing
[réiliŋ]

n. 난간, 울타리
A fence made from metal bars is called a railing or railings.

frighten복습
[fraitn]

v. 놀라게 하다, 섬뜩하게 하다; 기겁하다
If something or someone frightens you, they cause you to suddenly feel afraid, anxious, or nervous.

scratch복습
[skrætʃ]

v. 긁다, 할퀴다; n. 할큄, 찰과상
If you scratch yourself, you rub your fingernails against your skin because it is itching.

mustache복습
[mʌ́stæʃ]

n. 코밑수염
A man's mustache is the hair that grows on his upper lip.

trap복습
[træp]

n. 덫, 함정; v. 함정에 빠뜨리다, 좁은 장소에 가두다
A trap is a device which is placed somewhere or a hole which is dug somewhere in order to catch animals or birds.

feast*
[fi:st]

v. 맘껏 먹다; n. 축제, 진수성찬
If you feast on a particular food, you eat a large amount of it with great enjoyment.

instrument**
[ínstrəmənt]

n. 악기; 기구, 도구
A musical instrument is an object such as a piano, guitar, or flute, which you play in order to produce music.

slip복습
[slip]

v. 살짝 나오다[들어가다]; 미끄러지다; 슬며시 두다
If you slip somewhere, you go there quickly and quietly.

crimson복습
[krímzən]

a. 진홍색의; n. 진홍색
Something that is crimson is deep red in color.

leap복습
[li:p]

v. (leapt/leaped–leapt/leaped) 껑충 뛰다, 뛰어넘다; n. 뜀, 도약
If you leap, you jump high in the air or jump a long distance.

ledge*
[ledʒ]

n. (창문 아래 벽에 붙인) 선반; 절벽에서 (선반처럼) 튀어나온 바위
A ledge is a narrow shelf along the bottom edge of a window.

drainpipe
[dréinpàip]

n. 배수관, 하수관
A drainpipe is a pipe attached to the side of a building, through which rainwater flows from the roof into a drain.

immediately**
[imí:diətli]

ad. 곧 바로, 즉시
If something happens immediately, it happens without any delay.

gouge
[gaudʒ]

n. 홈, 구멍; (나무에 홈을 파는 데 쓰는) 둥근끌; v. 파내다, 찌르다
A gouge is a groove or hole made by digging with a pointed object.

unease ^{복습}
[ʌníːz]

n. 불안, 걱정 (uneasily ad. 불안 속에, 걱정하며)
If you have a feeling of unease, you feel rather anxious or afraid, because you think that something is wrong.

plot *
[plat]

vt. 꾀하다, 계획하다; n. 음모, 계획; 줄거리
If people plot to do something or plot something that is illegal or wrong, they plan secretly to do it.

ponder ^{복습}
[pándər]

v. 숙고하다, 깊이 생각하다
If you ponder something, you think about it carefully.

windowpane ^{복습}
[wíndoupèin]

n. 창유리
A windowpane is a piece of glass in the window of a building.

tablecloth ^{복습}
[téiblklɔːθ]

n. 식탁[테이블]보
A tablecloth is a cloth used to cover a table.

drawer ^{복습}
[drɔːr]

n. 서랍
A drawer is part of a desk, chest, or other piece of furniture that is shaped like a box and is designed for putting things in.

prod
[prɑd]

v. 쑤시다, 찌르다; 자극하다; n. 찌르기, 찌름
If you prod someone or something, you give them a quick push with your finger or with a pointed object.

disposable
[dispóuzəbl]

a. 사용 후 버릴 수 있는, 1회용의; n. 일회용 물품
A disposable product is designed to be thrown away after it has been used.

admit ^{복습}
[ədmít]

v. 인정하다
If you admit that something bad, unpleasant, or embarrassing is true, you agree, often unwillingly, that it is true.

protect ^{복습}
[prətékt]

v. 보호하다, 막다, 지키다 (protective a. 지키는, 보호하는)
To protect someone or something means to prevent them from being harmed or damaged.

coloration ^{복습}
[kʌləréiʃən]

n. (생물의) 천연색
The coloration of an animal or a plant is the colors and patterns on it.

jug ^{복습}
[dʒʌg]

n. 물주전자, 물병
A jug is a container with a handle and is used for holding and pouring liquids.

wasteland ^{복습}
[wéistlænd]

n. 황무지, 불모지
A wasteland is an area of land on which not much can grow or which has been spoiled in some way.

drive ^{복습}
[draiv]

n. (주택의) 진입로; 자동차 여행; v. 운전하다; 몰아가다
A drive is a wide piece of hard ground, or sometimes a private road, that leads from the road to a person's house.

crawl ^{복습}
[krɔːl]

vi. 기어가다, 느릿느릿 가다; n. 기어감; 서행
When you crawl, you move forward on your hands and knees.

hedge*
[hedʒ]

n. 산울타리, 울타리; v. 산울타리를 두르다, 둘러싸다
A hedge is a row of bushes or small trees, usually along the edge of a garden, field, or road.

roundabout
[ráundəbàut]

a. 멀리 도는, 우회적인; 넌지시 하는, 간접의; n. 에움길; 완곡한[간접적인] 말씨
If you go somewhere by a roundabout route, you do not go there by the shortest and quickest route.

dilapidate
[dilǽpidèit]

v. 황폐하게 하다; (건물 등을) 헐다, 헐어지다 (dilapidated a. 황폐한, 파손된)
To dilapidate means to fall or cause to fall into ruin or decay.

sway복습
[swei]

v. 흔들(리)다, 동요하다; 설득하다; n. 동요, 지배
When people or things sway, they lean or swing slowly from one side to the other.

plank*
[plæŋk]

n. 널, 두꺼운 판자
A plank is a long, flat, rectangular piece of wood.

edge복습
[edʒ]

n. 가장자리, 변두리, 끝; v. 조금씩[살살] 움직이다[이동시키다]; 테두리를 두르다
The edge of something is the place or line where it stops, or the part of it that is furthest from the middle.

meadow복습
[médou]

n. 목초지, 초원
A meadow is a field which has grass and flowers growing in it.

astonish복습
[əstániʃ]

vt. 깜짝 놀라게 하다 (astonishingly ad. 놀랍게도)
If something or someone astonishes you, they surprise you very much.

grunt복습
[grʌnt]

vi. (사람이) 툴툴거리다; (돼지가) 꿀꿀거리다; n. 꿀꿀[툴툴]거리는 소리
If you grunt, you make a low sound, especially because you are annoyed or not interested in something.

sweat복습
[swet]

v. 땀 흘리다; 습기가 차다; n. 땀
When you sweat, drops of liquid comes through your skin.

reveal복습
[riví:l]

vt. 드러내다, 보이다, 나타내다
If you reveal something that has been out of sight, you uncover it so that people can see it.

damp복습
[dæmp]

a. 축축한; n. 습기
Something that is damp is slightly wet.

slippery복습
[slípəri]

a. 미끄러운, 미끈거리는
Something that is slippery is smooth, wet, or oily and is therefore difficult to walk on or to hold.

spread복습
[spred]

v. 펴다, 펼치다, 퍼지다; 뿌리다; n. 퍼짐, 폭, 넓이
If you spread something somewhere, you open it out or arrange it over a place or surface, so that all of it can be seen or used easily.

well복습
[wel]

n. 우물; v. 솟아 나오다, 내뿜다, 분출하다
A well is a hole in the ground from which a supply of water is extracted.

retrace
[ri:tréis]

vt. 되돌아가다, 발자취를 따라가다; 회고하다, 회상하다
If you retrace your steps or retrace your way, you return to the place you started from by going back along the same route.

148

dangle
[dǽŋgl]

v. 매달(리)다; n. 매달린 것
If something dangles from somewhere or if you dangle it somewhere, it hangs or swings loosely.

string^{복合}
[striŋ]

n. 끈, 줄, 실; v. 묶다, 매달다, 꿰다
String is thin rope made of twisted threads, used for tying things together or tying up parcels.

infect*
[infékt]

v. 감염시키다, 전염시키다 (infected a. (세균에) 감염된)
To infect people, animals, or plants means to cause them to have a disease or illness.

bless^{복合}
[bles]

vt. 축복하다, 은총을 내리다
When someone such as a priest blesses people or things, he asks for God's favor and protection for them.

occur**
[əkə́:r]

vi. 생각이 떠오르다; 일어나다, 생기다
If a thought or idea occurs to you, you suddenly think of it or realize it.

confident**
[kɑ́nfidənt]

a. 자신만만한, 확신하는 (confidentially ad. 은밀히)
If a person or their manner is confident, they feel sure about their own abilities, qualities, or ideas.

confidential*
[kɑ̀nfədénʃəl]

a. 은밀한, 기밀의 (confidentially ad. 은밀히)
If you talk to someone in a confidential way, you talk to them quietly because what you are saying is secret or private.

extraordinary*
[ikstrɔ́:rdənèri]

a. 보기 드문, 비범한; 기이한, 놀라운
If you describe something or someone as extraordinary, you mean that they have some extremely good or special quality.

amble
[ǽmbl]

vi. 천천히[한가로이] 걷다
When you amble, you walk slowly and in a relaxed manner.

undergrowth
[ʌ́ndərgròuθ]

n. (큰 나무 밑의) 덤불, 풀숲
Undergrowth consists of bushes and plants growing together under the trees in a forest.

pace^{복合}
[peis]

n. 걷는 속도; 1보(의 거리), 보폭; 걸음걸이
If you keep pace with someone who is walking or running, you succeed in going as fast as them, so that you remain close to them.

whistle^{복合}
[hwisl]

v. 휘파람 불다; n. 휘파람; 호각
When you whistle or when you whistle a tune, you make a series of musical notes by forcing your breath out between your lips, or your teeth.

twitchy
[twitʃi]

a. 불안해[초조해]하는
If you are twitchy, you are behaving in a rather nervous way that shows you feel anxious and cannot relax.

witchy
[witʃi]

a. 마녀같은; 마법에 의한, 마법을 생각케 하는
A witchy person looks or behaves like a witch.

saunter
[sɔ́:ntər]

vi. 산책하다, 어슬렁거리다
If you saunter somewhere, you walk there in a slow, casual way.

hardly^{복습}
[háːrdli]

ad. 거의 ~아니다, 전혀 ~않다
You use hardly to modify a statement when you want to emphasize that it is only a small amount or detail which makes it true, and that therefore it is best to consider the opposite statement as being true.

tremble^{복습}
[trembl]

v. 떨다, 떨리다
If you tremble, you shake slightly because you are frightened or cold.

relieve^{복습}
[rilíːv]

vt. 안도하게 하다; (긴장 · 걱정 등을) 덜다 (relieved a. 안심한, 안도한)
If something relieves an unpleasant feeling or situation, it makes it less unpleasant or causes it to disappear completely.

relief^{복습}
[rilíːf]

n. 안심, 안도
If you feel a sense of relief, you feel happy because something unpleasant has not happened or is no longer happening.

lean^{복습}
[liːn]

① v. 상체를 굽히다, 기울다; 의지하다; ~을 기대어 세우다 ② a. 야윈, 마른
When you lean in a particular direction, you bend your body in that direction.

collapse[*]
[kəlǽps]

v. 무너지다, 붕괴하다; 쓰러지다, 맥없이 주저앉다; n. 무너짐, 붕괴
If a building or other structure collapses, it falls down very suddenly.

invisible^{복습}
[invízəbl]

a. 보이지 않는, 볼 수 없는
If you describe something as invisible, you mean that it cannot be seen, for example because it is transparent, hidden, or very small.

chatter^{복습}
[tʃǽtər]

v. 수다를 떨다, 재잘거리다; (공포 · 추위로 이가) 딱딱 맞부딪치다
If you chatter, you talk quickly and continuously, usually about things which are not important.

scamper^{복습}
[skǽmpər]

vi. 재빨리 달리다, 날쌔게 움직이다
When people or small animals scamper somewhere, they move there quickly with small, light steps.

pretend^{복습}
[priténd]

v. ~인 체하다, 가장하다; a. 가짜의, 꾸민
If you pretend that something is the case, you act in a way that is intended to make people believe that it is the case, although in fact it is not.

spill[*]
[spil]

v. 엎지르다, 흘리다; n. 엎지름, 유출
If a liquid spills or if you spill it, it accidentally flows over the edge of a container.

skitter
[skítər]

v. 잽싸게 미끄러지다, 경쾌하게 나아가다
If something skitters, it moves about very lightly and quickly.

chitter^{복습}
[tʃítər]

v. 지저귀다; (추워서) 떨다
To chitter means to twitter or chirp.

rush^{복습}
[rʌʃ]

n. 돌진, 급습; 혼잡, 쇄도; v. 서두르다, 돌진하다
A rush is a situation in which you need to go somewhere or do something very quickly.

scrabble^{복습}
[skrǽbl]

v. 헤적여 찾다, 긁어모으다; 휘갈겨 쓰다, 낙서하다; n. 휘갈겨 쓰기, 낙서
If you scrabble for something, especially something that you cannot see, you move your hands or your feet about quickly and hurriedly in order to find it.

150

stump ^{복습}
[stʌmp]

n. (나무의) 그루터기; 잘리고 남은 부분; vt. (발부리를) 차이다
A stump is a small part of something that remains when the rest of it has been removed or broken off.

crab ^{복습}
[kræb]

n. 게
A crab is a sea creature with a flat round body covered by a shell, and five pairs of legs with large claws on the front pair.

triumphant ^{복습}
[traiʌmfənt]

a. 의기양양한; 크게 성공한, 큰 승리를 거둔
Someone who is triumphant has gained a victory or succeeded in something and feels very happy about it.

clack
[klæk]

vi. 찰칵 소리를 내다; 재잘재잘 지껄이다; n. 찰칵하는 소리; 수다
If things clack or if you clack them, they make a short loud noise, especially when they hit each other.

momentum ^{복습}
[mouméntəm]

n. 기세, 여세
If a process or movement gains momentum, it keeps developing or happening more quickly and keeps becoming less likely to stop.

tumble ^{복습}
[tʌmbl]

v. 굴러 떨어지다, 넘어지다[뜨리다]; n. 추락; 폭락
If someone or something tumbles somewhere, they fall there with a rolling or bouncing movement.

muffle ^{복습}
[mʌfl]

vt. (소리를) 죽이다, 억제하다; 덮다, 싸다; n. 덮개
If something muffles a sound, it makes it quieter and more difficult to hear.

splash ^{복습}
[splæʃ]

n. 첨벙 하는 소리; (잉크 등의) 방울, 얼룩; v. (물·흙탕 물을) 튀(기)다, 첨벙거리다
A splash is the sound made when something hits water or falls into it.

daylight ^{복습}
[déilàit]

n. 낮; 일광, 빛
Daylight is the time of day when it begins to get light.

haul ^{복습}
[hɔːl]

v. 잡아끌다, 끌어당기다; 운반하다; 체포하다
If you haul something which is heavy or difficult to move, you move it using a lot of effort.

stalk ^{복습}
[stɔːk]

① vi. 활보하다, 으스대며 걷다; 살그머니 다가가다, 몰래 접근하다
② n. 줄기, 잎자루
If you stalk somewhere, you walk there in a stiff, proud, or angry way.

curl ^{복습}
[kəːrl]

vt. 꼬다, 곱슬곱슬하게 하다; n. 컬, 곱슬머리
If your toes, fingers, or other parts of your body curl, or if you curl them, they form a curved or round shape.

tip ^{복습}
[tip]

① n. (뾰족한) 끝 ② v. 기울이다; 뒤집(히)다 ③ n. 팁, 사례금
The tip of something long and narrow is the end of it.

spring ^{복습}
[spriŋ]

v. (sprang–sprung) 튀다, 뛰어오르다; n. 뜀, 뛰어오름; 샘, 수원지; (계절) 봄
When a person or animal springs, they jump upward or forward suddenly or quickly.

wiggle ^{복습}
[wigl]

v. (몸을) 뒤흔들다, (좌우로) 움직이다; n. 뒤흔듦
If you wiggle something or if it wiggles, it moves up and down or from side to side in small quick movements.

ecstatic
[ekstǽtik]

a. 무아지경의, 황홀한; 열광적인 (ecstatically **ad.** 희열에 넘쳐)
If you are ecstatic, you feel very happy and full of excitement.

tickle복습
[tikl]

vt. 간지럼을 태우다, 간질이다; **n.** 간지럼
If a part of the body tickles, or if something tickles it, it feels slightly uncomfortable and you want to rub it.

belly재습
[béli]

n. 배, 복부
The belly of a person or animal is their stomach or abdomen.

purr복습
[pəːr]

v. (기분 좋은 듯이) 그르렁거리다, 부르릉 하는 소리를 내다; **n.** 그르렁거리는 소리
When a cat purrs, it makes a low vibrating sound with its throat because it is contented.

contented*
[kənténtid]

a. (~에) 만족한 (contentedly **ad.** 만족하여)
If you are contented, you are satisfied with your life or the situation you are in.

patch복습
[pætʃ]

n. 부분, 단편, 파편; 헝겊 조각; 반창고; **v.** 헝겊을 대고 깁다
A patch on a surface is a part of it which is different in appearance from the area around it.

clap복습
[klæp]

v. 가볍게 치다[두드리다]; 박수를 치다
When you clap something, you strike it with the flat of the hand, usually in a friendly way as in encouragement or greeting.

savior*
[séivjər]

n. 구조자, 구제자
A savior is a person who saves someone or something from danger, and who is regarded with the veneration of a religious figure.

respect**
[rispékt]

n. 존경, 경의; 주의, 관심; **v.** 존경하다, 소중히 여기다
If you have respect for someone, you have a good opinion of them.

parlor재습
[páːrlər]

n. 거실, 응접실; 영업실
A parlor is a room in a house where people can sit and talk and relax.

grateful재습
[gréitfəl]

a. 고맙게 여기는, 감사하는
If you are grateful for something that someone has given you or done for you, you have warm, friendly feelings toward them and wish to thank them.

barely복습
[béərli]

ad. 간신히, 가까스로; 거의 ~않다
You use barely to say that something is only just true or only just the case.

retire복습
[ritáiər]

v. 퇴직하다, 물러나다, 은퇴하다
When older people retire, they leave their job and usually stop working completely.

lie복습
[lai]

vi. (lay–lain) 눕다, 누워 있다; 놓여 있다, 위치하다
If you are lying somewhere, you are in a horizontal position and are not standing or sitting.

entire재습
[intáiər]

a. 전체의; 완전한 (entirely **ad.** 완전히, 전적으로)
You use entire when you want to emphasize that you are referring to the whole of something, for example, the whole of a place, time, or population.

152

term**
[tə:rm]

n. 기간, 임기, 학기; 용어; 조건
A term is one of the periods of time that a school, college, or university divides the year into.

apprehensive
[æ̀prihénsiv]

a. 우려하는, 염려하는; 이해가 빠른, 총명한
Someone who is apprehensive is afraid that something bad may happen.

fancy^{복습}
[fǽnsi]

v. 공상[상상]하다; 좋아하다; **n.** 공상; 기호, 선호; **a.** 화려한, 고급스러운
To fancy means to feel a desire or liking for, to imagine.

press^{복습}
[pres]

v. 누르다, 밀어 누르다; 강요하다; **n.** 언론, 출판물; 누름, 압박
If you press something somewhere, you push it firmly against something else.

drift^{복습}
[drift]

v. 표류하다, 떠돌다; **n.** 표류; 경향, 추세
When something drifts somewhere, it is carried there by the movement of wind or water.

수고하셨습니다!

드디어 끝까지 다 읽으셨군요! 축하드립니다! 여러분은 이 책을 통해 총 30,640개의 단어를 읽으셨고, 900개 이상의 어휘와 표현들을 익히셨습니다. 이 책에 나온 어휘는 다른 원서를 읽을 때에도 빈번히 만날 수 있는 필수 어휘들입니다. 이 책을 읽었던 경험은 비슷한 수준의 다른 원서들을 읽을 때 큰 도움이 될 것입니다. 이제 자신의 상황에 맞게 원서를 반복해서 읽거나, 오디오북을 들어 볼 수 있습니다. 혹은 비슷한 수준의 다른 원서를 찾아 읽는 것도 좋습니다. 일단 원서를 완독한 뒤에 어떻게 계속 영어 공부를 이어갈 수 있을지, 도움말을 꼼꼼히 살펴보고 각자 상황에 맞게 적용해 보세요!

리딩(Reading)을 확실하게 다지고 싶다면? 반복해서 읽어 보세요!

리딩 실력을 탄탄하게 다지고 싶다면, 같은 원서를 2~3번 반복해서 읽을 것을 권합니다. 같은 책을 여러 번 읽으면 지루할 것 같지만, 꼭 그렇지도 않습니다. 반복해서 읽을 때 처음과 주안점을 다르게 두면, 전혀 다른 느낌으로 재미있게 읽을 수 있습니다.

처음 원서를 읽을 때는 생소한 단어들과 스토리로 인해 읽으면서 곧바로 이해하기가 매우 힘들 수 있습니다. 전체 맥락을 잡고 읽어도 약간 버거운 느낌이지요. 하지만 반복해서 읽기 시작하면 달라집니다. 일단 내용을 파악한 상황이기 때문에 문장 구조나 어휘의 활용에 더 집중하게 되고, 조금 더 깊이 있게 읽을 수 있습니다. 좋은 표현과 문장을 수집하고 메모할 만한 여유도 생기게 되지요. 어휘도 많이 익숙해졌기 때문에 리딩 속도에도 탄력이 붙습니다. 처음 읽을 때는 '내용'에서 재미를 느꼈다면, 반복해서 읽을 때에는 '영어'에서 재미를 느끼게 되는 것입니다. 따라서 리딩 실력을 더욱 확고하게 다지고자 한다면, 같은 책을 2~3회 정도 반복해서 읽을 것을 권해 드립니다.

리스닝(Listening) 실력을 늘리고 싶다면?
귀를 통해서 읽어 보세요!

많은 영어 학습자들이 '리스닝이 안 돼서 문제'라고 한탄합니다. 그리고 리스닝 실력을 늘리는 방법으로 무슨 뜻인지 몰라도 반복해서 듣는 '무작정 듣기'를 선택합니다. 하지만 뜻도 모르면서 무작정 듣는 일에는 엄청난 인내력이 필요합니다. 그래서 대부분 며칠 시도하다가 포기해 버리고 말지요.

따라서 모르는 내용을 무작정 듣는 것보다는 어느 정도 알고 있는 내용을 반복해서 듣는 것이 더 효과적인 듣기 방법입니다. 그리고 이런 방식의 듣기에 활용할 수 있는 가장 좋은 교재가 오디오북입니다.

리스닝 실력을 향상하고 싶다면, 이 책에서 제공하는 오디오북을 이용해서 듣는 연습을 해 보세요. 활용법은 간단합니다. 일단 책을 한 번 완독했다면, 오디오북을 통해 다시 들어 보는 것입니다. 휴대 기기에 넣어 시간이 날 때 틈틈이 듣는 것도 좋고, 책상에 앉아 눈으로는 텍스트를 보며 귀로 읽는 것도 좋습니다. 이미 읽었던 내용이라 이해하기가 훨씬 수월하고, 애매했던 발음들도 자연스럽게 교정할 수 있습니다. 또 성우의 목소리 연기를 듣다 보면 내용이 더욱 생동감 있게 다가와 이해도가 높아지는 효과도 거둘 수 있습니다.

반대로 듣기에 자신 있는 사람이라면, 책을 읽기 전에 처음부터 오디오북을 먼저 듣는 것도 좋은 방법입니다. 귀를 통해 책을 쭉 읽어보고, 이후에 다시 눈으로 책을 읽으면서 잘 들리지 않았던 부분들을 보충하는 것이지요.

중요한 것은 내용을 따라가면서, 내용에 푹 빠져서 반복해 들어야 한다는 것입니다. 이렇게 연습을 반복해서 눈으로 읽지 않은 책이라도 '귀를 통해' 읽을 수 있을 정도가 되면, 리스닝으로 고생하는 일은 거의 없을 것입니다.

 왼쪽의 QR코드를 스마트폰으로 인식하여 정식 오디오북을 들어 보세요! 더불어 롱테일북스 홈페이지(www.longtailbooks.co.kr)에서도 오디오북 MP3 파일을 다운로드 받을 수 있습니다.

스피킹(Speaking)이 고민이라면? 소리 내어 읽어 보세요!

스피킹 역시 많은 학습자들이 고민하는 부분입니다. 스피킹이 고민이라면, 원서를 큰 소리로 읽는 낭독 훈련(Voice Reading)을 해 보세요!

'소리 내어 읽는 것이 말하기에 정말로 도움이 될까?'라고 의아한 생각이 들 수도 있습니다. 하지만 인간의 두뇌 입장에서 봤을 때, 성대 구조를 활용해서 '발화'한다는 점에서는 소리 내어 읽기와 말하기에 큰 차이가 없다고 합니다. 소리 내어 읽는 것은 '타인의 생각'을 전달하고, 직접 말하는 것은 '자신의 생각'을 전달한다는 차이가 있을 뿐, 머릿속에서 문장을 처리하고 조음기관(혀와 성대 등)을 움직여 의미를 만든다는 점에서 같은 과정인 것이지요. 따라서 소리 내어 읽는 연습을 꾸준히 하는 것은 스피킹 연습에 큰 도움이 됩니다.

소리 내어 읽기를 하는 방법은 간단합니다. 일단 오디오북을 들으면서 성우의 목소리를 최대한 따라 하며 같이 읽어 보세요. 발음뿐 아니라 억양, 어조, 느낌까지 완벽히 따라 한다고 생각하면서 소리 내어 읽습니다. 따라 읽는 것이 조금 익숙해지면, 옆의 누군가에게 이 책을 읽어 준다는 생각으로 소리 내어 계속 읽어 나갑니다. 한 번 눈과 귀로 읽었던 책이기 때문에 보다 수월하게 진행할 수 있고, 자연스럽게 어휘와 표현을 복습하는 효과도 거두게 됩니다. 또 이렇게 소리 내어 읽은 것을 녹음해서 들어 보면 스스로에게도 좋은 피드백이 됩니다.

최근 말하기가 강조되면서 소리 내어 읽기가 크게 각광을 받고 있기는 하지만, 그렇다고 소리 내어 읽기가 무조건 좋은 것만은 아닙니다. 책을 소리 내어 읽다 보면, 무의식적으로 속으로 발음을 하는 습관을 가지게 되어 리딩 속도 자체는 오히려 크게 떨어지는 현상이 발생할 수 있습니다. 따라서 빠른 리딩 속도가 중요한 수험생이나 고학력 학습자들에게는 소리 내어 읽기가 적절하지 않은 방법입니다. 효과가 좋다는 말만 믿고 무턱대고 따라 하기보다는 자신의 필요에 맞게 우선순위를 정하고 원서를 활용하는 것이 좋습니다.

라이팅(Writing)까지 욕심이 난다면? 요약하는 연습을 해 보세요!

원서를 라이팅 연습에 직접적으로 활용하는 데에는 한계가 있지만, 적절히 활용하면 원서도 유용한 라이팅 자료가 될 수 있습니다.

특히 책을 읽고 그 내용을 요약하는 연습은 큰 도움이 됩니다. 요약 훈련의 방식도 간단합니다. 원서를 읽고 그날 읽은 분량만큼 혹은 책을 다 읽고 전체 내용을 기반으로, 책 내용을 한번 요약하고 나의 느낌을 영어로 적어보는 것입니다.

이때 그 책에 나왔던 단어와 표현을 최대한 활용하여 요약하는 것이 중요합니다. 영어 표현력은 결국 얼마나 다양한 어휘로 많은 표현을 해 보았느냐가 좌우하게 됩니다. 이런 면에서 내가 읽은 책을, 그 책에 나온 문장과 어휘로 다시 표현해 보는 것은 매우 효율적인 방법입니다. 책에 나온 어휘와 표현을 단순히 읽고 무슨 말인지 아는 정도가 아니라, 실제로 직접 활용해서 쓸 수 있을 만큼 확실하게 익히게 되는 것이지요. 여기에 첨삭까지 받을 수 있는 방법이 있다면 금상첨화입니다.

이러한 '표현하기' 연습은 스피킹 훈련에도 그대로 적용될 수 있습니다. 책을 읽고 그 내용을 3분 안에 다른 사람에게 영어로 말하는 연습을 해 보세요. 순발력과 표현력을 기르는 좋은 훈련이 될 것입니다.

꾸준히 원서를 읽고 싶다면? 뉴베리 수상작을 계속 읽어 보세요!

뉴베리 상이 세계 최고 권위의 아동 문학상인 만큼, 그 수상작들은 확실히 완성도를 검증받은 작품이라고 할 수 있습니다. 특히 '쉬운 어휘로 쓰인 깊이 있는 문장'으로 이루어졌다는 점이 영어 학습자들에게 큰 호응을 얻고 있습니다. 이렇게 '검증된 원서'를 꾸준히 읽는 것은 영어 실력 향상에 큰 도움이 됩니다.

아래에 수준별로 제시된 뉴베리 수상작 목록을 보며 적절한 책들을 찾아 계속 읽어 보세요. 꼭 뉴베리 수상작이 아니더라도 마음에 드는 작가의 다른 책을 읽어 보는 것 또한 아주 좋은 방법입니다.

• 영어 초보자도 쉽게 읽을 만한 아주 쉬운 수준. 소리 내어 읽기에도 아주 적합. Sarah, Plain and Tall*(Medal, 8,331단어), The Hundred Penny Box (Honor, 5,878단어), The Hundred Dresses*(Honor, 7,329단어), My Father's Dragon (Honor, 7,682단어), 26 Fairmount Avenue (Honor, 6,737단어)

• 중·고등학생 정도 영어 학습자라면 쉽게 읽을 수 있는 수준. 소리 내어 읽기에도 비교적 적합한 편.

Because of Winn-Dixie★(Honor, 22,123단어), What Jamie Saw (Honor, 17,203단어), Charlotte's Web (Honor, 31,938단어), Dear Mr. Henshaw (Medal, 18,145단어), Missing May (Medal, 17,509단어)

• 대학생 정도 영어 학습자라면 무난한 수준. 소리 내어 읽기에 적합하지 않음.

Number The Stars★(Medal, 27,197단어), A Single Shard (Medal, 33,726단어), The Tale of Despereaux★(Medal, 32,375단어), Hatchet★(Medal, 42,328단어), Bridge to Terabithia (Medal, 32,888단어), A Fine White Dust (Honor, 19,022단어), Jennifer, Hecate, Macbeth, William McKinley and Me, Elizabeth (Honor, 23,266단어)

• 원서 완독 경험을 가진 학습자에게 적절한 수준. 소리 내어 읽기에 적합하지 않음.

The Giver★(Medal, 43,617단어), From the Mixed-Up Files of Mrs. Basil E. Frankweiler (Medal, 30,906단어), The View from Saturday (Medal, 42,685단어), Holes★(Medal, 47,079단어), Criss Cross (Medal, 48,221단어), Walk Two Moons (Medal, 59,400단어), The Graveyard Book (Medal, 67,380단어)

뉴베리 수상작과 뉴베리 수상 작가의 좋은 작품을 엄선한 「뉴베리 컬렉션」에도 위 목록에 있는 도서 중 상당수가 포함될 예정입니다.

★「뉴베리 컬렉션」으로 이미 출간된 도서

어떤 책들이 출간되었는지 확인하려면, 지금 인터넷 서점에서 뉴베리 컬렉션을 검색해 보세요.

뉴베리 수상작을 동영상 강의로 만나 보세요!

영어원서 전문 동영상 강의 사이트 영서당(yseodang.com)에서는 뉴베리 컬렉션 『Holes』, 『Because of Winn-Dixie』, 『The Miraculous Journey of Edward Tulane』, 『Wayside School 시리즈』 등의 동영상 강의를 제공하고 있습니다. 뉴베리 수상작이라는 최고의 영어 교재와 EBS 출신 인기 강사가 만난 명강의! 지금 사이트를 방문해서 무료 샘플 강의를 들어 보세요!

'스피드 리딩 카페'를 통해 원서 읽기 습관을 길러 보세요!

일상에서 영어를 한마디도 쓰지 않는 비영어권 국가에서 살고 있는 우리가 영어 환경에 가장 쉽고, 편하고, 부담 없이 노출되는 방법은 바로 '영어원서 읽기'입니다. 언제 어디서든 원서를 붙잡고 읽기만 하면 곧바로 영어를 접하는 환경이 만들어지기 때문이지요. 하루에 20분씩만 꾸준히 읽는다면, 1년에 무려 120시간 동안 영어에 노출될 수 있습니다. 이러한 이유 때문에 영어 교육 전문가들이 영어 원서 읽기를 추천하는 것이지요.

하지만 원서 읽기가 좋다는 것을 알아도 막상 꾸준히 읽는 것은 쉽지 않습니다. 그럴 때에는 13만 명 이상의 회원을 보유한 국내 최대 원서 읽기 동호회 〈스피드 리딩 카페〉(cafe.naver.com/readingtc)를 방문해 보세요.

원서별로 정리된 무료 PDF 단어장과 수준별 추천 원서 목록 등 유용한 자료는 물론, 뉴베리 수상작을 포함한 다양한 원서의 리뷰와 정보를 무료로 확인할 수 있습니다. 특히 함께 모여서 원서를 읽는 '북클럽'은 중간에 포기하지 않고 원서 읽기 습관을 기르는 데 큰 도움이 될 것입니다.

Answer Key

chapter one

1. B   Coraline's family didn't own all of the house—it was too big for that. Instead they owned part of it.

2. C   "It's Coraline. Not Caroline. Coraline," said Coraline. … "I asked you not to call me Caroline. It's Coraline."

3. A   Coraline didn't think there really was a mouse circus. She thought the old man was probably making it up.

4. B   So Coraline set off to explore for it, so that she knew where it was, to keep away from it properly.

5. B   That was how she spent her first two weeks in the house—exploring the garden and the grounds.

6. D   The drawing room was where the Joneses kept the expensive: and uncomfortable) furniture Coraline's grandmother had left them when she died. Coraline wasn't allowed in there.

7. C   "You didn't lock it," said Coraline. Her mother shrugged. "Why should I lock it?" she asked. "It doesn't go anywhere."

chapter two

1. C   Miss Spink was walking her dogs. "Hello, Caroline," said Miss Spink. "Rotten weather."

2. B   "I do hope she doesn't get lost—it'll bring on her shingles if she does, you'll see," said Miss Forcible.

3. A   "The mice have a message for you," he whispered. Coraline didn't know what to say. "The message is this. Don't go through the door."

4. D   Coraline crept into the drawing room and tried to open the old door in the

corner. It was locked once more. She supposed her mother must have locked it again.

5. C   "You know, Caroline," she said, after a while, "you are in terrible danger."

6. D   There was a tiny china duck, a thimble, a strange little brass coin, two paper clips and a stone with a hole in it. She passed Coraline the stone with a hole in it.

chapter three

1. C   They went to the department store to buy the school clothes.

2. A   "… Nobody's got green gloves. I could be the only one."

3. C   "I'd better dash down to the shops and get some fish fingers or something," said her mother. "Do you want to come?"

4. B   It opened on to a dark hallway. The bricks had gone as if they'd never been there.

5. C   Only her skin was white as paper. Only she was taller and thinner. Only her fingers were too long, and they never stopped moving, and her dark red fingernails were curved and sharp. "Coraline?" the woman said. "Is that you?" And then she turned around. Her eyes were big black buttons.

6. B   It was the best chicken that Coraline had ever eaten. Her mother sometimes made chicken, but it was out of packets or frozen, and was very dry, and it never tasted of anything.

7. A   It wasn't a pretty song. Coraline was sure she'd heard it before, or something like it, although she was unable to remember exactly where.

chapter four

1. B   Or almost exactly the same: around Miss Spink and Miss Forcible's door were blue and red lightbulbs that flashed on and off spelling out words, the lights chasing each other around the door. On and off, around and around.

2. B   Half of her wanted to be very rude to it; the other half of her wanted to be polite and deferential. The polite half won.

3. C   "I can see that. Well, how did you get here?" "Like you did. I walked," said the cat. "Like this." Coraline watched as the cat walked slowly across the lawn. It walked behind a tree, but didn't come out the other side.

4. A   Miss Forcible threw the knife at the balloon. It popped loudly, and the knife

stuck into the board just above Coraline's head and twanged there. Coraline breathed out.

5. B   "If you want to stay," said her other father, "there's only one little thing we'll have to do, so you can stay here for ever and always." They went into the kitchen. On a china plate on the kitchen table was a spool of black cotton, and a long silver needle, and, beside them, two large black buttons.

6. D   Coraline took a deep breath and stepped into the darkness, where strange voices whispered and distant winds howled. She became certain that there was something in the dark behind her: something very old and very slow.

chapter five

1. B   She tried to put the bunch of keys back on top of the door again. She tried four or five times before she was forced to accept that she just wasn't big enough, and she put them down on the counter next to the door.

2. C   "She's vanished under mysterious circumstances," said Coraline, "and I believe my father has as well." "I'm afraid we'll be out all day tomorrow, Caroline, luvvy," said Miss Forcible. "We'll be staying with April's niece in Royal Tunbridge Wells."

3. A   The cat stared at her. Then it walked out into the hall. She followed it. It walked the length of the corridor and stopped down at the very end, where a full-length mirror hung… The mirror showed the corridor behind her; that was only to be expected. But reflected in the mirror were her parents. They stood awkwardly in the reflection of the hall.

4. A   "You ask your mother to make you a big old mug of hot chocolate, and then give you a great big old hug. There's nothing like hot chocolate and a hug for making the nightmares go away. And if she starts to tell you off for waking her up at this time of night, why you tell her that that's what the policeman said."

5. D   In the mirror it was daytime already. Coraline was looking at the hallway, all the way down to her front door. The door opened from the outside and Coraline's mother and father walked inside. They carried suitcases.

6. C   "Why don't you have your own key on this side?" asked Coraline. "There is only one key. Only one door," said the other father.

7. A   "Challenge her. There's no guarantee she'll play fair, but her kind of thing loves games and challenges."

chapter six

1. B   For a moment she felt utterly dislocated. She did not know where she was; she was not entirely sure who she was.

2. C   "Out," he told her. "Fixing the doors. There are some vermin problems." He seemed pleased to have somebody to talk to.

3. B   "Really, I mustn't talk to you when she's not here," he said. "But don't you worry. She won't be gone often."

4. A   But there was something else, something she did not remember seeing before. A ball of glass, up on the mantelpiece above the fireplace. She went over to the fireplace, went up on tiptoes, and lifted it down. It was a snow globe, with two little people in it.

5. A   "She may try," said the cat, unimpressed. ... "There's ways in and ways out of places like this that even she doesn't know about."

6. D   "You may come out when you've learned some manners," said the other mother. "And when you're ready to be a loving daughter."

chapter seven

1. C   It was the size of a broom closet: tall enough to stand in or to sit in, not wide or deep enough in which to lie down. One wall was glass, and it felt cold to the touch. She went around the room a second time, running her hands over every surface that she could reach, feeling for doorknobs or switches or concealed catches—some kind of way out— and founding nothing. A spider scuttled over the back of her hand and she choked back a shriek.

2. D   "The names are the first things to go, after the breath has gone, and the beating of the heart. We keep our memories longer than our names. ..."

3. B   "She stole our hearts, and she stole our souls, and she took our lives away, and she left us here, and she forgot about us in the dark."

4. D   "Aye. And hidden them." "That is why we could not leave here, when we died. She kept us, and she fed on us, until now we've nothing left of ourselves, only snakeskins and spider husks. Find our secret hearts, young mistress."

5. A   "She won't keep me in the dark forever," said Coraline. "She brought me here to play games. Games and challenges, the cat said. I'm not much of a challenge here in the dark."

6. C   And as she fell asleep she thought she felt a ghost kiss her cheek, tenderly, and

a small voice whisper into her ear, a voice so faint it was barely there at all, a gentle wispy nothing of a voice so hushed that Coraline could almost believe she was imagining it. "Look through the stone," it said to her.

chapter eight

1. C   The other mother carried Coraline into the kitchen and put her down very gently upon the countertop. Coraline struggled to wake herself up, conscious only for the moment of having been cuddled and loved, and wanting more of it, then realizing where she was and who she was with.

2. B   "There were other children in there," she said. "Old ones, from a long time ago." "Were there?" said the other mother.

3. D   "If I lose I'll stay here with you forever and I'll let you love me. I'll be a most dutiful daughter. I'll eat your food and play Happy Families. And I'll let you sew your buttons into my eyes."

4. C   "An exploring game," suggested Coraline. "A finding-things game."

5. A   "I put her in there myself. And when I found her trying to crawl out, I put her back." "Swear on something else. So I can trust you to keep your word."

6. D   The gray glass marble from the bottom of the toy box sat, dully, in the pink palm of her hand. She raised the stone to her eye once more and looked through it at the marble. Once again the marble burned and flickered with a red fire.

7. B   She realized then that, terrifying though the thing on the wall that had once been the other Misses Spink and Forcible was, it was attached to the wall by its web, encased in its cocoon. It could not follow her.

chapter nine

1. D   It was true: the other mother loved her. But she loved Coraline as a miser loves money, or a dragon loves its gold. In the other mother's button eyes, Coraline knew that she was a possession, nothing more. A tolerated pet, whose behavior was no longer amusing.

2. B   "But if you wanted to get into the flat in the front—the empty one—to look around, you would find the door locked, and then where would you be?" ... "Here," she said. "You'll need this to get in." She tossed the key, casually, toward Coraline, who caught

164

it, one-handed, before she could think about whether she wanted it or not.

3. A　"Poor thing," she said. "I bet she made you come down here as a punishment for telling me too much." The thing hesitated, then it nodded.

4. A　"Poor thing," she said. "You're just a thing she made and then threw away."

5. B　"Run, child. Leave this place. She wants me to hurt you, to keep you here forever, so that you can never finish the game and she will win. She is pushing me so hard to hurt you. I cannot fight her."

6. D　As the thing reached her, Coraline put out her hand and closed it around the thing's remaining button eye and she tugged as hard as she knew how. For a moment nothing happened. Then the button came away and flew from her hand, clicking against the brick wall before it fell to the cellar floor.

7. A　It's listening for me, thought Coraline. I must be extra quiet. She took another step up, and her foot slipped on the step, and the thing heard her.

chapter ten

1. D　This place smelled as if all the exotic foods in the world had been left out to go rotten.

2. B　She could not truly make anything, decided Coraline. She could only twist and copy and distort things that already existed.

3. D　"We will listen to you and play with you and laugh with you. Your other mother will build whole worlds for you to explore, and tear them down every night when you are done. Every day will be better and brighter than the one that went before. …"

4. A　Coraline took a step closer to the man, and he fell apart. Black rats leapt from the sleeves and from under the coat and hat, a score or more of them, red eyes shining in the dark. They chittered and they fled.

5. C　It was as bad as the summer that her mother had taken the training wheels off Coraline's bicycle; but then, back then, in with all the cuts and scrapes (her knees had had scabs on top of scabs) she had had a feeling of achievement. She was learning something, doing something she had not known how to do. Now she felt nothing but cold loss.

6. C　Beside the decapitated rat, a smug expression on its face, was the black cat. It rested one paw on the gray glass marble.

7. B　"What's wrong?" asked Coraline. "They've gone," said the cat. "They aren't there anymore. The ways in and out of this place. They just went flat."

chapter eleven

1. C   "So you're back," said the other mother. She did not sound pleased. "And you brought vermin with you." "No," said Coraline. "I brought a friend,"

2. B   It was funny, Coraline thought. The other mother did not look anything at all like her own mother.

3. A   "Why don't you open it?" said Coraline. "They'll be there, all right." It was her only way home, she knew. But it all depended on the other mother's needing to gloat, needing not only to win but to show that she had won.

4. A   And, hard as she could, she threw the black cat toward the other mother. It yowled and landed on the other mother's head, claws flailing, teeth bared, fierce and angry. Fur on end, it looked half again as big as it was in real life.

5. D   The other people in the corridor—three children, two adults—were somehow too insubstantial to touch the door. But their hands closed about hers, as she pulled on the big iron door handle, and suddenly she felt strong.

6. B   The wall she was touching felt warm and yielding now, and, she realized, it felt as it were covered in a fine downy fur. It moved, as if it were taking a breath. She snatched her hand away from it.

7. C   The cat looked up at her, then rested its head on her hand, licking her fingers with its sandpapery tongue. It began to purr. "Then we're friends?" said Coraline.

chapter twelve

1. B   She pushed her hands into the pockets of her dressing gown, and she pulled out three marbles, a stone with a hole in it, the black key, and an empty snow globe.

2. B   Coraline took a piece of string from her toy box, and she strung the black key on the string. Then she knotted the string and hung it around her neck.

3. C   He put the computer to sleep, stood up, and then, for no reason at all, he picked Coraline up, which he had not done for such a long time, not since he had started pointing out to her she was much too old to be carried, and he carried her into the kitchen.

4. A   She was at a picnic, under an old oak tree, in a green meadow. The sun was high in the sky and while there were distant, fluffy white clouds on the horizon, the sky above her head was a deep, untroubled blue.

5. D   Coraline knew it was a dream then, because none of them ever got tired or

166

winded or out of breath. She wasn't even sweating.

6. C   "I'm just pleased it's all over," said Coraline. … "There's a but, isn't there?" said Coraline. "I can feel it. Like a rain cloud." … "Yes, Miss." "But I got you three back," said Coraline. "I got Mum and Dad back. I shut the door. I locked it. What more was I meant to do?"

7. A   There was a pause, then the whatever it was scuttled away down the hall. There was something odd and irregular about its footsteps, if they were footsteps. Coraline found herself wondering if it was perhaps a rat with an extra leg. . . .

chapter thirteen

1. B   Coraline's parents never seemed to remember anything about their time in the snow globe. At least, they never said anything about it, and Coraline never mentioned it to them.

2. C   She sat up, and lifted the pillow. The fragments of the glass marbles that she saw looked like the remains of eggshells one finds beneath trees in springtime: like empty, broken robin's eggs, or even more delicate—wren's eggs, perhaps.

3. D   "I think he was in some sort of fight," said Miss Spink. "He has a deep gash in his side, poor dear. We'll take him to the vet later this afternoon. I wish I knew what could have done it."

4. A   Coraline slept uneasily that night, waking from time to time to plot and plan and ponder, then falling back into sleep, never quite certain where her pondering ended and the dream began, one ear always open for the sound of something scratching at her windowpane or at her bedroom door.

5. C   And then the weight and the momentum of the hand sent the plastic dolls' cups flying, and the paper tablecloth, and the key, and the other mother's right hand went tumbling down into the darkness of the well.

6. B   "The mice tell me that all is good," he said. "They say that you are our savior, Caroline."

7. C   Normally, on the night before the first day of term, Coraline was apprehensive and nervous. But, she realized, there was nothing left about school that could scare her anymore.

Coraline

1판 1쇄   2012년   8월   1일
2판 3쇄   2024년   7월 22일

지은이   Neil Gaiman
기획   이수영
책임편집   김보경 차소향 이수영
콘텐츠제작및감수   롱테일 교육 연구소
저작권   명채린
디자인   김덕오
마케팅   두잉글 사업 본부

펴낸이   이수영
펴낸곳   롱테일북스
출판등록   제2015-000191호
주소   04033 서울특별시 마포구 양화로 113, 3층(서교동, 순흥빌딩)
전자메일   help@ltinc.net

ISBN 979-11-91343-94-6 14740